WARRENPOINT

SERGEANT DENIS DONOGHUE

WARRENPOINT

Denis Donoghue

SYRACUSE UNIVERSITY PRESS

Copyright © 1990 by Denis Donoghue

All Rights Reserved

Syracuse University Press Edition 1994

94 95 96 97 98 99   6 5 4 3 2 1

This book was originally published by Alfred A. Knopf, Inc.,
1990.

The paper used in this publication meets the minimum require-
ments of American National Standard for Information Sciences
—Permanence of Paper for Printed Library Materials, ANSI
Z39.48-1984. ∞™

Library of Congress Cataloging-in-Publication Data
Donoghue, Denis.
    Warrenpoint / Denis Donoghue. — 1st ed.
        p. cm. — (Irish studies)
    Originally published: New York : Knopf, 1990.
    ISBN 0-8156-0303-7 (pbk.)
        1. Warrenpoint (Northern Ireland)—Social life and customs.
    2. Fathers and sons—Northern Ireland—Biography.
    3. Intellectuals—Northern Ireland—Biography. 4. Critics—
    Northern Ireland—Biography. 5. Donoghue, Denis.
    I. Title. II. Series: Irish studies (Syracuse, N.Y.)
    [DA995.W3D66 1994]
    941.6′58—dc20   94-29282

Manufactured in the United States of America.

For John,

who died

WARRENPOINT

JOHN DONOGHUE

I THINK OF IT AS A TOWN, not as a village. In my private dictionary a village is a community surrounded by fields: the people are farmers, or they serve farmers and their families as shopkeepers, nurses, doctors, teachers, priests. At Sunday Mass the men wear caps, not hats, and after Mass they stand around the church to chat, gossip, or stare at the hills. A town, small or large, is not dependent upon the land that surrounds it; it opens on a different world. Tullow, in County Carlow, where I was born on December 1, 1928, still seems to me a village. No disrespect is intended. When I stand outside my brother Tim's shop—boots and shoes—in Bridge Street, I smell cows. On one side of Tullow there is Rathvilly, a village, and farther still, in the direction of Dublin, there is Baltinglass, another village, though it regards itself as a town. In the other direction Carlow is a town, because it is big enough to make you forget the fields surrounding it. One street in Carlow leads to another much the same: it is the kind of town that Yeats hated, though he probably never saw it. He saw many towns like Carlow and passed through them with distaste—Mullingar, Athlone, Athenry, I suppose—on his way to Coole Park, Lady Gregory's estate in Gort, County Galway.

Warrenpoint is a town because one side of it opens upon the sea. If you look at a map of Ireland, find Belfast, come around the Ards Peninsula and Strangford Lough, and mark Ardglass, Newcastle, Kilkeel, and Rostrevor, you'll find the next town is Warrenpoint, where Carlingford Lough narrows till it ceases being a lough at Narrow Water and becomes the Newry Canal; not much of a canal these days. Warrenpoint looks across the lough to Omeath, a meagre town though it has Newry on one side and Carlingford on the other and the Cooley Mountains behind it and one of the mountains is called the Long Woman's Grave. Warrenpoint is in Northern Ireland; Omeath is in the South. A ship of the British Navy now sits in the middle of the lough to prevent incursions of the Irish Republican Army, deemed to be rampant in the woods and villages between Omeath and Dundalk. Weapons, bought in Holland or otherwise acquired in Libya, are somehow delivered to the IRA in the North. A few of these deliveries are probably made by small boats at night from Omeath or Carlingford, despite the vigilance of the Navy. In my time such vigilance was not required. We had a dock, and coal boats regularly arrived with supplies for Kelly's Coalyard, but there was no cause to assume that the cargoes included guns.

Warrenpoint was a seaside resort, if you please. I don't recall that the local Urban District Council displayed coloured pictures advertising the charm of the town; nothing like "Come to Sunny Prestatyn" in Philip Larkin's poem, with a laughing girl in a swimsuit and, behind her, hotels with palm trees expanding from her thighs and arms. Nothing as grand as that. As a resort, Warrenpoint relied not upon laughing girls or golden weather but upon three more reliable considerations. One: you could get to the place easily from any part of the North by train, since it was the terminus of the Great Northern Railway's branch line from Newry. No longer; the train is gone. Two: Warrenpoint has the largest square in Ireland, a great place for amusements, circuses, swings and roundabouts, ice-cream carts, parades, celebrations. The square was promiscuous in the wiles of display. Three: the licensing laws for the sale of alcohol are stricter in the North than in the South, mainly because Presbyterians keep the Sabbath more severely than Catholics do. If you came to Warrenpoint for a Sunday trip, you would find the public houses shut, but you could go by ferryboat across to Omeath, an open town on the Sabbath, for drink and noise. Meanwhile, children and their mothers passed the Sunday on a rough pebble beach in Warrenpoint and watched the yachts and rowing boats in the lough. If the pleasure of watching other people enjoying themselves wore off, the mothers could walk to the town park and see their betters playing tennis. Or walk along the coast road to Rostrevor, a smaller and prettier town than Warrenpoint and socially several cuts above it. Warrenpoint had tea shops, but Rostrevor had the Great Northern Hotel, a place of emphasised elegance. Not now: it was decisively bombed some years ago by the IRA, and the remains of it have been removed.

I REMEMBER NOTHING before Warrenpoint:

> *I remember, I remember*
> *The house where I was born,*
> *The little window where the sun*
> *Came peeping in at morn.*

I don't, unfortunately. It was customary for an expectant mother in my mother's time to go back to her own people for several weeks before and after the birth of the child. My mother's family was divided in two parts. Some of the children were reared with their parents in Clonmel, County Tipperary, and some with more remote relatives in Tullow. My mother and her sister Ciss grew up in Tullow, so she went back there when her time came. Whether I was born in the house in Bridge Street or in the local cottage hospital, I don't know. Probably in the house, a big ramshackle affair containing a shop, run by Martin Coady, my mother's uncle. The shop was reputed to have sold, during the few years of its splendour, more bacon than any other shop in the east of Ireland. In my time it sold virtually nothing but bacon and, for specially favoured customers, butter and cigarettes. Martin Coady, a man of relentless gloom, as I recall him, was also the local representative of the Graguenamanagh Sack-Hiring Company, and he had a barn behind the shop where he spent the winter days mending torn sacks in preparation for the harvest season. Silently he spread the damaged part of a sack across his knees and darned it with a large, curved sacking needle and thick brown twine. I watched him till my silence, matching his, became oppressive to both of us. Meanwhile Ciss attended to the shop. She did not stand behind the counter but sat in the little sitting room reading the sporting page of *The Irish Independent* and choosing two horses to back for a double. She never attended a race or learned anything about horses, but she took advice from *The Irish Independent*'s racing correspondent and waited for the day on which both of the chosen horses would win. A double would make her fortune, or so she thought. During the racing season she put a wager on two horses every day and, since it was not respectable for a lady to enter a bookmaker's premises, sent me there to place the bet. Except for the great occasion on which, like everyone else in Ireland, she backed Lovely Cottage to win at Galway, she regularly lost her bet. But her mild little gamble passed the time: most of the morning was spent picking the horses, the afternoon held the excitement of waiting for the result, and at least an hour or two in the evening she spent wondering what had gone wrong.

In any case, I give my place of birth as c/o Martin Coady, Bridge Street, Tullow, County Carlow, Ireland.

Tullow comes into the reckoning because my father, a policeman in the Royal Irish Constabulary, was stationed there when he met my mother, a girl named Johanna O'Neill. Her father, too, was in the RIC, stationed in Clonmel. My father was promoted to the rank of sergeant in Tullow when the reigning sergeant, named Morris, went mad and ran from the barracks, for reasons known only to himself. My father was the man in the gap and he got the job, the only preferment he ever enjoyed. When the Government of Ireland Act (1920) divided Ireland into two parts, with a parliament in Belfast to govern the six northern counties, it was ordained that any member of the RIC would have the right to go North and take up the same rank in the newly formed Royal Ulster Constabulary. My father, having seen enough of Ireland and of police work in a violent time, spent two months trying to find an alternative job. He and my mother went to Chester, where he tried to establish himself as an insurance agent, till someone started a rumour that he had murdered a man in Ireland and was "on the run." My father gave up and went to Northern Ireland to take his rank in the RUC. He always maintained that the lapse of five months in his official career, taken in association with his Catholicism, made any further promotion in the RUC impossible. I believe him. During his years in the RUC it was not yet necessary for the authorities to show goodwill toward Catholics or to promote them above the rank of sergeant. If my father had been twenty or thirty years younger and in the same profession, he would probably have been selected as a token Catholic and raised perhaps to the rank of Head Constable or even District Inspector to placate the natives. In the event, he retired on pension before such a concession became necessary. "Too late, too late, he cried in vain."

MY FATHER WAS BORN in a mountainy cottage in County Kerry. If you go from Killarney toward Tralee, and turn off the main road into the Black Valley and keep going till the road ends and you can go no farther except on foot, you'll come to three or four houses in a townland—not decisive enough to be a village—called Cloghernoosh: the postal address is Cloghernoosh, Beaufort, Killorglin, near Killarney, County Kerry. The stone walls of my father's house are still there, but the roof is gone. My father's father never made a living from the few square yards of land he owned or the few sheep he put on the mountain. He earned some extra pounds by renting a horse to visitors, mostly American tourists, who wanted to cross the Gap of Dungloe from Kate Kearney's Cottage, and by rowing the same or other tourists around one of the lakes of Killarney. We never learned what happened, how it came about that he was drowned, along with the several Americans he had in the boat. My father was twelve at the time and the eldest of several children. The family survived, and as the children grew up, they emigrated to America, most of them getting jobs in the vicinity of Watertown, Massachusetts. The first time I came to America, to teach at the Harvard summer school, my father's sister Mary, whom I had never met in Ireland, entertained me as if I were a conquering hero. Which in some sense I felt myself to be. I was a professor. She had emigrated to Watertown, found a job in the local telephone exchange, married an ice vendor named Torres, and developed a fairly lucrative skill in interior decoration. Her brothers lived in the environs of Watertown. I don't know about other sisters, except for one, who disappeared in America for many years and was not heard of till, after her death, we heard that she had left America, gone to England, and worked as a priest's housekeeper in Hastings. There was a photograph of her in the parlour of the barracks in Warrenpoint, and I gathered from my father that she had in some way gone wrong. Evidently not. Nothing wrong with a priest's housekeeper; it's a decent occupation.

IN WARRENPOINT WE LIVED in the police barracks, or rather in half of it, the other half being given over to the official business of the police, centred on what was called the Day Room. There was a thick concrete wall about six feet from the building, protecting it against an attack or a riot. By locking two small gates and one large one, you could close off the barracks and hold out against a siege. The barracks had two cells, or lockups, as they were called, one for men, one for women. I remember my father lifting me up to look through a metal slit at a man he had arrested. The cell had a wooden platform instead of a bed, a small barred window good enough to let in a dim light, and a drain in the corner so that the cell did not need to be cleaned; it could be hosed out instead. It smelled of a strong disinfectant, and the walls were whitewashed. In a smaller room beside the stairs there was a wooden chest filled with revolvers, rifles, hand grenades, and tear-gas canisters for the dispersal of crowds.

Behind the barracks there was a parade ground for the constables, and behind that a garden of sorts, which housed for protection the telephone exchange for Warrenpoint and the surrounding district.

My father was in charge of seven or eight regular constables and about the same number of part-time policemen, called B-Specials, whom I hated and feared because they were, to a man, Protestants and Unionists. In 1920 an armed force of Special Constabulary was established. Special Constables were Protestants, recruited mainly from the Orange Order, a body of extreme loyalists, as we would now call them, formed at the end of the eighteenth century to celebrate forever the victory of William, Duke of Orange, over King James II at the Battle of the Boyne on July 1, 1690. The remainder of the Special Constabulary was recruited from the Ulster Volunteer Force, a paramilitary body ready to take up arms to prevent the formation of a united, independent Ireland. Special Constables were divided into three categories: A's, who served as full-time policemen; B's, men who had ordinary jobs in the towns of the North but also served as part-time uniformed and armed policemen; and C's, a militia ready to be called up for emergencies. The A's and C's were soon disbanded, but the B-Specials remained in force and could become full-time policemen if necessary. In 1922 sectarian conflict in the North resulted in 230 deaths, and a new armed police force was established, the Royal Ulster Constabulary, to deal with the situation. In theory, one-third of the RUC were to be Catholics, but in the event, few Catholics joined. The RUC was obviously a Protestant organization, its chief aim to keep Catholics in check. The fact that my father was one of the few Catholics who joined the force is easily explained: he had no choice, no other job was available, and the RUC could not reject his application.

The B-Specials are still in force as auxiliaries to the RUC, but now they are called the Ulster Defence Regiment and are part of the British Army.

Our half of the barracks, the "married quarters," had a parlour, a kitchen and scullery, three bedrooms, a bathroom, and an outhouse. The parlour had a black upright piano, a circular mahogany table, and a trolley for the wireless. There were two photographs on the wall above the piano. One showed my father and mother, shortly after their wedding, I suppose. He is in the uniform of a sergeant in the RIC: he sports a moustache, firmly twisted at the ends, unwaxed but as if waxed. He is sitting on a high-backed chair; stern, un-yielding, as if nothing but duty called him. My mother is standing beside him. Both are facing the camera. She is wear-ing a long dark skirt, a white blouse, and a small brooch. Her hair is tied in a bun, her face resolute, unsmiling. Her right hand is placed upon my father's left shoulder; a marriage declared come what might. The photograph is oval, blurred at the edges; the frame is oblong. Husband and wife: my parents are looking at the world in that relation, answerable to a civic as well as to a religious contract.

The second photograph showed my father's sister, the one we thought had gone wrong. She had a blouse much like my mother's, tight to the neck, its severity mitigated by a circle of lace. She was not looking at the camera but in profile, off to the left, as if already planning to emigrate.

A third photograph was not, as I recall, fixed to the wall, but it stood in a small case on the piano. It is a photograph of my younger brother, John, the one who didn't survive an attack of pneumonia. He is in his pram, smiling. The pho-tograph was taken in the gap between the barracks and the protective wall. John died when he was fourteen months old. That left four of us: Tim, my sisters Kathleen and May; I was now the youngest. I recall my father, on the day of John's funeral, carrying the little coffin down the stairs. I wasn't allowed to go to the funeral: three days after Christmas, 1932, if my memory is accurate on this point. I was sent across the street to the Heatleys, neighbours though not intimate friends, while the funeral procession walked from the church to the graveyard at Burren, a mile and a half above the town. I stayed at the Heatleys', fingering the piano. I never heard John mentioned again in our family, except by my sisters many years later, when my parents were dead. In Ireland, and perhaps in other countries, a dead child is either talked about in the family as if still alive or is never mentioned again after the funeral.

MARY DOUGLAS has a paragraph in *Natural Symbols* about the decencies of working-class homes:

> The first thing that is striking about the English working class home is the attempt to provide privacy in spite of the difficulties of layout. The respect for the privacy of bodily functions corresponds to the respect for the distinction between social and private occasions; the back of the house is appropriately allocated to cooking, washing and excretory functions; the front parlour, distinguished from the living room-kitchen, is functionless except for public, social representation. Space by no means wasted, it is the face of the house, which speaks composedly and smiles for the rest of the body; from this room a person must rush if he bursts into tears.*

*Mary Douglas, *Natural Symbols: Explorations in Cosmology* (London: Barrie and Rockliff, 1970), p. 158.

Our house was similar and different. It was continuous with the official half of the building. There was no visible separation between the dayroom of the barracks and the sergeant's married quarters. As such, it presented an image of authority to the town by being larger than it had to be and by appearing to be entirely official. The wall that ran along the entire front of the barracks, breached only by an iron gate in front of the main door, enhanced the implication of authority but also made one wonder at the need of it. It seemed at once assertive and vulnerable: else why did it think it necessary to assert its authority?

The married quarters were different in certain respects from the ordinary working-class home. The kitchen and the parlour were at the front of the house, equally in view if they could have been seen behind the barrier of the wall. The common life was conducted in the kitchen, and the parlour was reserved for special occasions. But many activities constituted a special occasion. Listening to the radio was special; so was the formal occasion of schoolwork. I did my lessons on the parlour table, which gleamed in preparation for the social life we rarely had. The smile to which Mary Douglas refers was displayed in the table, the piano, and the radio. So it was a serious matter when I spilled a bottle of ink on the table and the stain could not be removed. It was concealed by a doily and on special occasions further concealed by a vase of flowers. The parlour was kept remote, however, by being reserved for these spiritually superior purposes.

Not that the comparison with an English working-class home should be forced. We were neither English nor working-class. Not working-class, because my father's hands did not need to become dirty: he was not a manual or an industrial worker; he used a pen and, more rarely, a telephone. I would say we were lower-middle-class Catholic, but my father's membership in the RUC raised him formally and professionally, if not socially. By being in uniform, he was better dressed than a lower-middle-class Catholic would normally be, and this made his social image somewhat ambiguous. Whether we wanted this to happen or not, some authority from the RUC adhered to us in our social lives. We were Sergeant Donoghue's family in a town that knew how to estimate such things.

WARRENPOINT HAD ITS SEASONS, but they were economic and political rather than natural. The rhythms of natural life were available, but the town did not appear to take account of them. The tide came in and went out. At certain times of the day one could walk along the stony beach, cross the breakwater—a device, this breakwater, to retain the small amount of sand in one section of the shoreline—and dig one's footprints into the sand. At other times the waves at that point came high enough to crash over the wall on the shore road. It was necessary to run to the other side of the road or get drenched. Walking up to Burren or along the shore road to Rostrevor, one saw evidence of the seasons: trees shed their leaves and in due course displayed new growth. But the town didn't seem to advert to these sequences: it did not sink into itself in winter, stir in spring, or burst into full sail with the summer. Or if it did, the reason was commercial, as if on principle, and natural only by coincidence. The town was made for crowds rather than for the individuals who came to Warrenpoint because it was there to be seen. We had a tourist season, a short summer constrained by the vagary of weather.

The climax of the year was "the marching season," the few weeks before and after the twelfth of July. The town prepared itself for the tourists, not to make them feel welcome in any personal sense but to give them the annual satisfaction of finding shops freshly painted, boats as merry as the waves, tea shops and ice-cream parlours pretending to be new. The tourist season over, the paint began to fall from the walls, the old concrete was allowed to yield to the wind and the salt spray. The town went out of season, waiting for another June, the trains, the hired buses. Behind the walls along the sea-front, the boarding houses, bed-and-breakfast places, lodging houses, private hotels, there may indeed have been private lives, walking to a different tune, beating time to entirely different rhythms, uncommercial and spontaneous. But it was hard to see the evidence. We seemed to have crowds, or we had nothing, least of all ourselves. Even those, like my family, who had no part in the mercenary life of the town, waited for it to come to life in the only form we knew: gregarious, haphazard, noisy.

APART FROM GIVING ME the bare details of his early life, my father didn't engage in reminiscence. So far as I could see, he was not unhappy or conscious of being disappointed, but he didn't bask in gone times or occasions. He was grimly related to the present tense and determined to gain a better future for his children, so he hadn't much time for nostalgia. He seemed to consider his life as merely a preparation for someone else's; mine, to be specific. He had an acute interest in the future, but it was my future rather than his. I find it strange, though, that he didn't take an interest in the harmless nostalgia of the photograph. Walter Benjamin has a memorable paragraph about photographs in one of his essays:

> In photography, exhibition value begins to displace cult value. . . . But cult value does not give way without resistance. It retires into an ultimate retrenchment: the human countenance. It is no accident that the portrait was the focal point of early photography. The cult of remembrance of loved ones, absent or dead, offers a last refuge for the cult value of the picture. For the last time the aura emanates from the early photographs in the fleeting expression of a human face. This is what constitutes their melancholy, incomparable beauty.*

But there is another profile to the face. Susan Sontag has noted, in her book on photography, that photography was hardly invented before it was used by the police in Paris for mug shots of criminals and suspected criminals. The aura, in those cases, belongs not to their melancholy beauty but to their air of desolation. In photography the portrait speaks of the sitters in their isolation, making them either beautiful or terrible in that capacity. Still, I wonder why my parents showed little or no interest in the possession of such images. Or why, in my turn, I haven't bothered to gather together the few photographs we had. My sister Kathleen, more given to such memorabilia than I have been, has retained them, including a school photograph of me, taken when I was about seven, my hair short and laid bare in a fringe, my cheeks tight as if testing the risk entailed by a smile.

My father showed no interest, so far as I know, in the possession of images. He did not need to look at his wedding

*Walter Benjamin, *Illuminations,* ed. Hannah Arendt, tr. Harry Zohn (New York: Schocken Books, 1969), p. 226.

photograph. As for the only known photograph of John, presumably he knew that, having seen it once, he would not need to consult it again. It still exists. Kathleen has it. When I see it, John smiling out of his pram, I think, with some irritation: What had he to smile about? But then I wonder: Why do I feel irritated?

Perhaps the explanation is that I am irritated by the signs of naiveté. The body is a naïf: among the tenses, it knows only the present. It can't even imagine a future, except notionally: debility, sluggishness, creaking limbs. A body in pain can't believe that it will ever be relieved of the pain: the present moment is the only condition it believes in. From the moment of his birth John was a child who would die after fourteen months, but he didn't know that. During those months his body was indifferent to a fate it couldn't foresee. It thought it would live forever. The smile, caught by the Brownie box camera and fixed in my mind so long as I recall it, is the sign of a child's body in its felicity. Let be.

In "The Philosophy of Composition," Poe decides that "melancholy is . . . the most legitimate of all the poetical tones" since "beauty of whatever kind, in its supreme development, invariably excites the sensitive soul to tears." The next question is: " 'Of all melancholy topics, what, according to the *universal* understanding of mankind, is the *most* melancholy?' " Death, obviously. " 'And when,' I said, 'is this most melancholy of topics most poetic?' " The answer is again obvious. " 'When it most closely allies itself to *Beauty:* the death, then, of a beautiful woman is, unquestionably, the most poetical topic in the world—and equally is it beyond doubt that the lips best suited for such topic are those of a bereaved lover.'" Poe's argument is convincing so long as it is designed to hold the perfection of poetic sentiment imprisoned in the lyric words. There is no reason why the lover's complaint should ever end or why he should want to escape from the poetic circle. But the death of a child had this advantage, as a poetic theme, over that of a beautiful woman: that intimations of waste, pointlessness, God's indifference, and so forth, prompt the mourner to practise an irony even in the enjoyment of such favours as he receives. The force willing to see a child die may strike again at any felicity. The sentiments of Mahler's *Kindertotenlieder* prompt the singer to retain a mental reservation even in the most extreme passage of mourning, enough to effect his escape from the song and to remind him that precaution is necessary. The German language is gifted in establishing, within a compound word, a narrative firm enough to point the speaker on his way beyond the sentiments phonetically linked. *Kindertotenlieder:* children, the dead, the songs the mourners sing.

"Now, just wash and brush up your memoirias a little bit."*

D O I R E M E M B E R accurately that our kitchen had brownish-red stone tiles, a gas cooker, an old cast-iron range, a wooden box for holding odds and ends, a sofa with the horsehair stuffing falling out of it and the springs sagged, a Singer sewing machine, four wooden chairs, and a linoleum-covered table with one corner of it broken or hacked off? Is that likely? What would make me certain of these things, as certain as I

*James Joyce, *Finnegans Wake* (London: Faber and Faber, 1939), p. 507.

am that in the scullery my father always kept a large bottle
of cod-liver oil and drank from it twice a day? And when I
refused to drink the stuff, he compromised by buying a bottle
of Kepler's malt, which contained enough cod-liver oil to
appease him and enough malt to remove the vile taste. I'm
not sure about the table, and yet I feel that I'm merely introducing a doubt as if miming a scruple I'd like to be seen
showing. The corner of the table was broken or hacked.
Which, I can't say. About the linoleum, I'm sure enough.
There is a curious passage in Nabokov's *Transparent Things*
where he says that "when we concentrate on a material object,
whatever its situation, the very act of attention may lead to
our involuntarily sinking into the history of that object":

> Novices must learn to skim over matter if they want it to
> stay at the exact level of the moment. Transparent things,
> through which the past shines.*

I am not sure that I understand him. What is that past which
shines through transparent things if it is not a sense or a
recollection of those things? And if it is, how can it be other
than their history? I can't distinguish between the past and
my sense of those objects which detain my mind. The difficulty is that the more I concentrate my mind on a particular
object, the more opaque it seems to become, as if it developed
its own personality by virtue of being noticed. Is this what
Hopkins means when he says, in one of the journals, that
what you look hard at seems to look hard at you? If I believed
Walter Pater, I would expect to find that when I think of the
kitchen table, I see it dissolving before my eyes into flickering
impressions, gone as soon as come, till nothing remains but
my sense of myself, my mind. But I don't find this at all.

*Vladimir Nabokov, *Transparent Things* (New York: Penguin Books, 1972), p. 7.

The table becomes opaque, almost sullen under my attention, as if it wanted nothing of my mind or interest. It's like taking a word, any word, and speaking it aloud, and repeating the word fifteen or twenty times, and then you find it recoiling from you as if your voice were a blow, and the meaning of it goes dead on you. Thinking of the table, I recall the linoleum, and the wetness of it when my mother cleaned it after a meal, and the stickiness of my hands on it, and my thumb as it traced the line of the broken part. Is that what Nabokov means by sinking into the history of an object? All I know is that the table doesn't dissolve into my impressions of it—Pater is wrong about that, anyway—but seems to return my stare, without welcoming my attention.

MY MOTHER WAS a minor presence in comparison with my father. I remember her as frail, delicate, never in good health for long. Every few weeks she suffered an attack of some kind. We were told it was epilepsy, and perhaps it was. Kathleen maintains that it was merely a symptom of hormonal imbalance. The immediate sign of an attack was a long, high-pitched wail, and then my mother would collapse. The important thing was to make sure that she didn't hurt herself. We were to remove her dentures, keep her well away from the stove, put a cushion under her head, and run for Mrs. Crawford. Mrs. Crawford, wife of Mr. Crawford the teacher, had been a nurse before she married. The Crawfords lived at Innisaimer, a few houses up Charlotte Street, and Mrs. Crawford would know what to do. We carried my mother up to bed and left her to the attention of adults for two days. When I went in to see her, she always said: "I suppose I gave you a fright the other night."

These attacks nearly always happened at night, except for one occasion, when my mother, Kathleen, and I went for a walk along the Mount Road, and my mother suddenly gave the wailing sign and fell. Generally, I associate the wail with darkness and with my father's absence on duty. There was something called a meet patrol, every few weeks, when my father would meet, by arrangement, the sergeants-in-charge of Rostrevor and Mayobridge to compare notes, pool their information on anything that might be going on in the area. I hated those occasions. My father always prepared for them in the same way: got his carbide lamp ready, pumped up the wheels of his bicycle, and set off, about midnight, long after bedtime. I dreaded the possibility that my mother would "get a turn," as we called it, while my father was out on this patrol. If I was asleep, maybe I wouldn't hear her and she might fling herself out of the bed and hurt herself on the floor. I still hear the hiss of the lamp and see my father's hand twisting the carbide container home.

I ASSUMED THAT my mother was as content as her circumstances allowed her to be. Her debility set clear limits upon her enjoyment of life: she could not be expected to dance. But within those constraints she seemed not unhappy. No question of psychological or spiritual import was deemed to arise. We were encouraged to believe that contentment depended upon one's health. "If you have your health," my mother used to say, "you'll be all right," and she had every right to an opinion on that matter. My father agreed that one's health was paramount: if you were not well, not sound in wind and limb, you could not face the world. But the question was not turned in my mother's direction. I assumed that facing the world was something my father would do for her and that he was well able to do it. She was provided for.

So far as I know, the most reliable sign of my mother's well-being was her humming a tune. When she was silent, it was impossible to know how she was feeling: she did not comment on the matter. But silence, over a period of several hours, was a bad sign: she might be thinking terrible thoughts. If she hummed a tune, all was well. She didn't sing the songs, she merely hummed a phrase here and there, as if quoting them. If she heard, on the radio, the supreme Irish tenor John McCormack singing "I Hear You Calling Me" or "Bless This House," she would hum bits of the songs over the following few days. When I heard her humming these snatches, I silently added the words as McCormack sang them:

> *I hear you calling me:*
> *You called me when the moon had raised her light.*
> *And so I went with you into the night.*
> *I hear you calling me.*

But the favourite song was "Bless This House," not because it sounded like a hymn but because McCormack's voice while singing it spoke of warmth and good-fellowship; it was like having turkey at Christmas and going to midnight Mass:

> *Bless this house, O Lord we pray,*
> *Keep it safe by night and day.*
> *Bless these walls, so firm and stout,*
> *Keeping want and trouble out.*
> *Bless the people here within,*

Keep them pure and free from sin.
Bless us all, that we may be,
Ever open to joy and love.

My father liked to hear my mother humming. It was a good sign. "She seems well, doesn't she?" On the evidence of a few bars of an old song. What she really felt about her life, we never thought or dared to ask.

MY MOTHER'S RIGHT ARM was noticeably thicker than her left. When she was a girl, she tended shop in her uncle Martin's place in Tullow, taking turns with Ciss. They did not have a bacon slicer or any other machine, only two large knives. I never saw my mother slicing rashers, but I saw Ciss engaging in the only shopkeeping mystery she practised. To keep the meat intact, you had to cut each slice fairly thick, and when you came to a bone, you had to use the knife as a hammer and break through it. It was a question of tact to decide how much bone and rind you put on the weighing scale. Generally, rind was left on the rashers, but most of the bone was discarded; all of it, for a favoured customer. The weighing scale had a white plate of heavy delft and a copper pan to hold the weights. It was my job to stack the weights in due order on the counter, starting with the four-pounder and going up to the smallest, half an ounce. No finer adjustment was possible: half an ounce tipped the scale one way or the other. My aunt then took pencil and a scrap of paper, worked out the price, and threw the scrap of paper into the till; the only form of bookkeeping she maintained.

Short-tempered and tetchy, Ciss dominated my mother in

the shop and throughout the house. It was taken for granted that whatever my mother did, she did badly. Not that Ciss liked to be interrupted in her day's work with *The Irish Independent* or her calculations on the racing page. My mother was welcome to the shop while Ciss was estimating the chances of a horse repeating, at Leopardstown on a dry day, its recent success at Mallow on heavy terrain. It was customary for the racing correspondent to supply the record of each horse's three previous performances, so Ciss had to decide whether a horse marked 030 might be ready to win or another one with better form—231, perhaps, or 301—might be too tired to try his best. If a customer arrived while Ciss was deep in such cogitations, my mother was summoned to attend to her, at whatever risk to domestic economy. But if Ciss had committed herself to a bet, she had nothing more to do and took command in the shop. My mother joined in the conversation but took no part in the business transactions. There were innumerable ways of making her feel redundant.

MY SOCKS WERE always too small for me, so I wore holes in them. My mother darned them, using a rounded block of wood to hold the sock where the heel should be. The wool was rarely the same colour as the sock. To conceal the darn, I pulled the sock so far down the sole of my foot that I wore a new hole an inch or two above the heel. When she sewed a button on my coat, there was no choice of thread: ink or boot polish confused the issue enough to make the coat presentable. We had a Singer sewing machine, which ran according to the speed with which my mother worked the spindle up and down. She could not achieve a straight line or adjust the patch to the hole it was supposed to cover. She was neither stupid nor indifferent, but the implements she had to use—cloth, thread, meat, vegetables, the gas cooker, the stove—were invariably at odds with her need of them.

THE CLONMEL BRANCH of my mother's family seemed to me socially superior to the Tullow branch, mainly because it included her brother Seamus. In the house at 13 Bolton Street, Clonmel, there was a photograph showing my mother's father, her sister Jenny, and Seamus. Her father was a tall, white-haired man, not as military in his bearing as my father was but still a well-made man. Jenny was as sharp in feature as in manner. Seamus received a far better education than his sisters: he became a teacher, taught in Rockwell College, a majestic place. It must have been a cause of dismay to his father—an RIC man—that Seamus was a fervent nationalist, a rebel, and in the years before the Easter Rising of 1916 second in command to Sean Treacy, leader of the IRA in south Tipperary. In the photograph his father is wearing a long frock coat of heavy serge, but Seamus is wearing Celtic garb, tasselled stockings, the kilt, cloak, and Tara brooch. I doubt if he ever held a gun; he mainly organised nationalist sentiment and maintained communications throughout the country. But he was ready to do whatever was required. In the event, the Easter Rising turned into a debacle everywhere except in Dublin, mainly because the leadership of the rebels was split between those led by Padraig Pearse, who wanted to go ahead with the Rising on Easter Monday, and those led by Eoin MacNeill, who thought it prudent to wait. Pearse took it upon himself to order his men to rise, but MacNeill countermanded the order. On Easter Sunday in Clonmel, Seamus did not know whether or not the Rising was to take place: one rumour displaced another. When news arrived that Pearse had proclaimed the Republic of Ireland from the General Post Office in Dublin, Seamus O'Neill went on the run, hiding out in the Gaeltacht in Ring. He wanted to see Ireland free and united in that freedom, but he cared even more deeply for the revival of the Irish language and Irish cultural forms than for the political independence of the country and its release from the British Empire. When he was arrested, he was jailed first in Dundalk, later in Lewes and Frongoch. When he was released, he gave up his political and military life, took no part in the Civil War. After the Treaty the new unarmed police force—the Garda Siochana—was established in the South, and there was need of educated men as officers. Seamus joined the force, was promoted in a matter of days to the rank of Inspector, and eventually became Superintendent in charge of Galway, mainly because Galway included certain Irish-speaking areas, notably the Aran Islands, and some court cases were conducted in Irish. When my sister Kathleen enrolled as a student in University College, Galway, she lodged with Seamus and his family in a fine house in Lower Salthill.

Being an educated man and an officer in the Garda, Seamus O'Neill was socially far superior to us, so a visit from him made a special occasion. He was always well dressed and spoke with a certain elegance. In deference to my mother, who did not know enough Irish to carry on a conversation, he spoke English, but when he and I were otherwise alone, he reverted to Irish, causing me a little difficulty, since his dialect was Munster and mine was Donegal. We corresponded without difficulty in Irish, the differences between the dialects arising mainly in the pronunciation of the words rather than in diction or spelling. He married an Irish poet, Una ni Cuidithe: one of the few books I owned was a small volume of her lyrics.

Seamus's nationalism was not an embarrassment to us. My father liked him well enough and respected the range of his education. It was silently agreed that we would talk of domestic matters, not of politics. We knew that he regarded the Civil War as a disaster from which the country had not recovered, but we did not pursue a sore topic. Besides, domestic matters, schooling, health, the cost of living, and the problem of acquiring an education and getting ahead in the world filled the available space. My mother, between policemen and a rebel brother, kept her own counsel. She was gifted in that respect.

FOR SOME REASON I go through my shoes unevenly: the right one is more heavily worn than the left. My father mended our shoes. He had an iron last, a hammer, pincers, boxes of nails and tacks. Always leather, except for the heels, which were rubber. His favourite leather was Dry-Ped, a pale-green substance thinner than ordinary leather but supposedly of harder grain. With a scissors, he cut a pattern of newspaper to fit the sole of each shoe, then cut—the knife curved as if already intent upon its chore—a channel in the Dry-Ped along the edge of the paper. Sometimes he steeped the leather in water for an hour or two, to make it supple. Then he nailed it carefully and finished it off with a rasp. I smeared the sides of the Dry-Ped with polish—but if my father had time, he would warm a piece of wax over a candle and work it into the new edges. Heels were easier to attach. The rubber was easier than the leather to cut. Some skill was required to ensure that the nails were driven down straight, so that they could not be seen on the surface. My father had a gadget for driving the nails a little farther into each hole of the heel: in a perfect piece of workmanship, no nail protruded or caved into a buckle. "There, now," my father said when the work was done, "that'll keep you off the street."

WHEN SHOULD ONE BEGIN to remember? I am dismayed to discover that the first three and a half years of my life are a blank. I remain sceptical about the powers of memory that other people claim, though in some cases the evidence is firm. One of my favourite books is Henry James's *A Small Boy and Others,* and my favourite chapter in it is the fifth. But one passage strains my credence. In 1848, at the age of five, James heard that Louis Philippe had fled to England. The news caused consternation in James's parents. "I had heard of kings presumably," James recalled, "and also of fleeing: but that kings had sometimes to flee was a new and striking image." He told his parents of a scene he recalled from his earliest presence in Paris:

> I had been there for a short time in the second year of my life, and I was to communicate to my parents later on that as a baby in long clothes, seated opposite to them in a carriage and on the lap of another person, I had been impressed with the view, framed by the clear window of the vehicle as we passed, of a great stately square surrounded with high-roofed houses and having in its centre a tall and glorious column. I had naturally caused them to marvel, but I had also, under cross-questioning, forced them to compare notes, as it were, and reconstitute the miracle.

The view, parents and the mature James agreed, was that of the Rue St.-Honoré, as the family crossed the Rue Castiglione and saw, "for all my time, the admirable aspect of the Place and the Colonne Vendôme."

Is this to be believed? James doesn't merely claim that at the age of two he saw the Colonne Vendôme, but that he was "impressed" by it. How could he know that the sensation he felt was one of finding something impressive? In comparison with what? The only evidence for his "observation of monumental squares" is that he couldn't have seen such things in New York or Albany or even in London, "which moreover I had known at a younger age still." I don't claim that James was a liar, but I can't believe that he remembered seeing the Colonne. Perhaps on one of the many occasions on which, in his adult years, he saw the scene, he happened to recall, as a very young child, travelling somewhere with his parents and someone else and looking through the carriage window. He then, for whatever reason, joined the two images in his mind and let the conjunction pass for a recollection. I refuse to believe that he was precocious enough to commit the scene to memory in his second year. Genius or no genius.

But the question is not simple. Within a page or two James makes the point that while his early life was spent in notably amiable circumstances and surrounded by warm-hearted people, "the scene on which we so freely bloomed does strike me, when I reckon up, as extraordinarily unfurnished." He doesn't explain: unfurnished in comparison with whose life? What it apparently comes to is that the members of the James family had, for company, one another and, in crucial addition, each had himself, his inward life:

How came it then that for the most part so simple we yet weren't more inane? This was doubtless by reason of the quantity of our inward life—ours of our father's house in especial I mean—which made an excellent, in some cases almost an incomparable, *fond* for a thicker civility to mix with when growing experience should begin to take that in. It was also quaint, among us, I may be reminded, to have *begun* with the inward life; but we began, after the manner of all men, as we could, and I hold that if it comes to that we might have begun much worse.

The supreme instance, for James, of the practice of the inward life was his father: admittedly he practised it in default of an outward life which might have included a proper degree of recognition among his peers. In the virtual absence of such recognition, he had no alternative but to concentrate his mind upon its inwardness:

> Of our father's perfect gift for practising *his* kind I shall have more to say; but I meanwhile glance yet again at those felicities of destitution which kept us, collectively, so genially interested in almost nothing but each other and which come over me now as one of the famous blessings in disguise.*

James is honourable enough to acknowledge that he, like his sister and brothers, and father and mother, could afford these felicities of destitution because his grandfather had left them enough money to enable them not to make a living but to rest upon one.

I WONDER ABOUT the status of things we forget. According to my family's history, I was brought to the Eucharistic Congress in Dublin in 1932. It was in the summer, in

*Henry James, *A Small Boy and Others* (New York: Scribner's, 1913), pp. 55ff.

Phoenix Park, and the Pope celebrated Mass, and McCormack sang "Panis Angelicus," and thousands of people came
from all over Ireland to take part in the ceremonies. I have
not the least recollection of being present. I was three years
and seven months old, and the whole episode is blank to me.
But I remember vividly John's death six months later. The
first thing I remember was a death in the family. Isn't it
strange that I developed—if that is the correct way of putting
it—the power of memory just in time to employ it upon the
first event worth remembering?

   I am told that I have a notable flair for not remembering,
especially when the forgotten, suppressed, or transcended
event reflected badly upon me at the time. It is not true. I cut
a poor enough figure, it seems to me, in many of the episodes
I recall. When have I ever been heroic?

I CAN'T BELIEVE that I have suppressed the experiences
I have forgotten or that they must have been painful if they
required such disposal. Many of the episodes I remember are
trivial and were even then trivial: the feeling of running my
fingers along the iron surface of the watering trough in the
square; the pleasure, while watching the coal boats at Kelly's
Coalyard being unloaded, of anticipating the moment at
which the huge buckets threw the coal on the pyramid; the
thrill of the day on which I graduated from short pants into
long ones and knew that my knees would no longer be on
display; the night on which Duffy's Circus played in the field
behind the barracks and my father got me a free seat on the
excuse of inspecting the ticketing arrangements. As for the

multitude of events I have forgotten: no matter, they can have amounted only to more of the same.

In Borges's "Funes the Memorious" we read this:

Locke, in the seventeenth century, postulated (and rejected) an impossible language in which each individual thing, each stone, each bird and each branch, would have its own name; Funes once projected an analogous language, but discarded it because it seemed too general to him, too ambiguous. In fact, Funes remembered not only every leaf of every tree, every tree of every wood, but also every one of the times he had perceived or imagined it. He decided to reduce each one of his past days to some 70,000 memories, which would then be defined by means of ciphers. He was dissuaded from this by two considerations: his awareness that the task was interminable, his awareness that it was useless. He thought that by the hour of his death he would not even have finished classifying all the memories of his childhood.

Borges claims for Funes "a certain stammering grandeur." An aura of nobility surrounds the project of enumeration, consistent with the satisfaction of knowing that Funes did not in the end proceed with it. The desire does him credit, since he proposed to be in the world but not to interfere with its objects and arrangements. Unfortunately, as Borges observes, "to think is to forget differences, generalise, make abstractions." In Funes's teaming world, "there were only details, almost immediate in their presence."* Much as I love Hopkins's poems, I find his nagging insistence on individuality, detail, and *haecceitas* tolerable only because he did it for the glory of God.

*Jorge Luis Borges, *Ficciones,* edited and with an Introduction by Anthony Kerrigan (New York: Grove Press, 1962), pp. 113–14.

L ET   M E   G E T a few dates straight. My father's date of birth is not known to me. It's hardly worth the labour of finding it in the Public Record Office or the Custom House. He joined the RIC on March 3, 1913. He and my mother married in Tullow on April 21, 1920. He left the RIC on disbandment of the force on April 11, 1922. They went to Chester on June 6, 1922, and stayed there unhappily till September. On September 28, 1922, he joined the RUC and left on pension on August 31, 1946. I think he was born on some date in March 1887; he died on August 15—the Feast of the Assumption of the Blessed Virgin—1957. So he was about thirty-three years old when he married. That seems reasonable: he did not do things in a hurry. Frances and I were married on my twenty-third birthday. My father thought I was far too young to be rushing into the responsibilities of matrimony, but he could not deny that according to his own criteria—a permanent and pensionable job in the Civil Service—I could afford to get married if I wanted to.

Certificate No. 18960

ROYAL IRISH CONSTABULARY.

Form 37/3

Certificate of Character.

On discharge of No. 67143, Sergeant Denis
Donoghue, who joined the above-named Force
on the 3rd. day of March 1913 and was discharged on the 11th. day of April 1922 in consequence of disbandment. His general conduct
during the period of his service was: very
good.

Description on Discharge.

Age: 35¹⁄₁₂ years.   Height: 5 ft. 9¾ inches.
Colour of hair: dark.   Colour of Eyes: grey.
Complexion: Fresh.
Special distinguishing marks (if any): nil.

Royal Irish Constabulary Office,
Dublin Castle,
16th. May, 1922.
Pension Number: 18438.

Ex-Sergeant Denis Donoghue is hereby informed that he has been awarded a Pension of

£111:3s.:0d. per annum, in respect of his service in the Royal Irish Constabulary, such pension to date from 11th. April, 1922.

Certificate No. 1274

ROYAL ULSTER CONSTABULARY.
Certificate of Character.

On discharge of No. 2807. Sergeant Denis Donoghue, who joined the above-named Force on the 28th day of September 1922 and was discharged on the 31st. Day of August 1946 in consequence of retirement on age limit. His general conduct during the period of his service was: very good.

Description on Discharge.

Age: 59½ yrs.　　　　Height: 5' 9¾"
Colour of Hair: Grey.　　Colour of Eyes: Grey
Complexion: Fresh.
Special distinguishing marks (if any): none.

Ministry of Home Affairs,
Stormont,
Belfast,
Northern Ireland,
19th. February, 1947.

Sir:

I am directed by the Minister of Home Affairs to enclose Forms of Declaration and an explanatory memorandum in connection with the Pensions (Increase) Act (N.I.), 1944, the provisions of which have been extended by the Expiring Laws Continuance Act (N.I.), 1946, for a further year to the 31st. December, 1947.

If you:—

(1) have reached the age of 60 years, or

(2) retired on account of physical or mental infirmity, or,

(3) are permanently incapacitated by physical or mental infirmity from engaging in any full-time employment, and your total income from all sources if you are single or a widower and have no dependants does not exceed £277 a year, or if you are married or being single or a widower have at least one dependant does not exceed £352 a year, you should complete the appropriate Declarations and return them to the Ministry.

I am, Sir,
Your obedient servant,
S. Birch (for Accountant)

I INQUIRED FROM Robin Sinclair, keeper of records in the RUC, about my father's service. It appears that, on joining the force, he was assigned to Arney, a village in County Fermanagh; before my time. Unless he was transferred to another station, he served in Arney from 1922 to 1928. He took up duty in Warrenpoint on November 1, 1928, exactly a month before I was born. I assume that my mother spent the summer and the autumn and most of the winter in Tullow, and that my father kept house in the barracks with May, Kathleen, and Tim. Robin Sinclair tells me that my father received two "favourable records" while serving in the RIC: one First Class, one Second Class. What could the qualitative difference be? Perhaps he put his life at risk and gained a First? In the RUC he gained another favourable record: some act of merit in 1930. Like every other policeman serving in July 1935, he received the King's Jubilee Medal. In 1936, according to Mr. Sinclair, my father received another favourable record in a case of sheep stealing. On June 13, 1932, he was appointed Explosives Inspector, but that did not mean a promotion; he was merely put in charge of explosives in Warrenpoint and empowered to see that they were properly stored and used. That's all. Her Majesty's Government has nothing further to say about my father. He performed well in a case of sheep stealing.

PHILIP LARKIN DESCRIBED his childhood as "a forgotten boredom," but it couldn't have been emphatic in both
respects. If it was boring, he remembered it in that character;
if he had forgotten it, he would not have remembered even
enough of it to call it boring. Besides, in the same poem,
"Coming," he says that with the coming of spring he feels

> *. . . like a child*
> *Who comes on a scene*
> *Of adult reconciling,*
> *And can understand nothing*
> *But the unusual laughter,*
> *And starts to be happy.*

How would he know that feeling unless he remembered having it or imagined what it would be like? And even if he only
imagined it, he must have known something like it. He
doesn't describe the laughter (high-pitched, quietly sensual,
tinkling, or whatever) but notes it as a memorable event, unusual because rare, not because it had any special sensory
mark.

There were no audible reconcilings between my mother
and father, either because they did not squabble or because
they kept their squabbles to themselves. I don't think they
were close enough to find it necessary to quarrel. The bound-
aries were set, agreed upon. My father drew the lines, traced
the maps. I recall only one occasion on which I came upon
them when they were doing something unusual. I happened
to go into their bedroom—it was broad day, long before bed-

time—and they were lying, fully clothed indeed but aslant on the bed. They could have been looking out the window, which was only a few inches higher than the bed. They weren't holding each other; or if they were, I have suppressed the image. But they moved apart immediately, as if caught in a compromising position, a gesture, if not an act. I did not feel jealous of him in relation to her. It is possible that I resented her being closer to him than I was; closer, at least for that occasion.

EVERY SUMMER WE WENT to Tullow and lived with Uncle Martin and Aunt Ciss. My father hired a hackney car and driver from McNulty's: a big Austin with two tip-up seats behind the front seat, and a back seat of leather. My father came with us for the drive and to release my mother from the chores of the road. If we had made the trip by train, we would have had to change, in Dublin, from Amiens Street to King's Bridge; from the Great Northern Railway to the Great Southern. The problems of bringing children across the city were thought to be too arduous for my mother. Besides, my father enjoyed the trip, spent one night with us in Tullow, and came back to Warrenpoint with the driver the following morning. He did not take a formal vacation. Summer was the busiest season in Warrenpoint, what with the holiday-makers and the day-trippers from Belfast, Portadown, and Bally-mena. My father had to be on hand for the marching season, when annually incited political passions went on display.

Meanwhile, in Tullow we walked up to the farm, helped to bring in the hay, swam in the Slaney at the Ouragh Rocks and Aghade, sunned ourselves on the bridge. On Sunday nights my mother, with Ciss, Moll Manzer, and the next-door O'Neills, walked the mile to Mrs. Dowling's, where they played cards and drank tea till midnight.

BIRTHDAYS WERE NOT CELEBRATED or even ac-knowledged. I never knew my father's birthday, or my moth-er's, or that of Tim or Kathleen or May; or even John's birthday, which might reasonably have been italicised by his death. My parents did not attach any significance to one day rather than to another. Sunday differed from Saturday because we went to Mass on Sunday and only to confession on Sa-turday night, but otherwise no day claimed privilege. The only recognised cadence among events was repetition; one day, then the next, and the next. Rilke says in *The Notebooks of Malte Laurids Brigge* that "one already knew, of course, that life took pleasure in making no distinctions." Mealtimes were the only punctuation marks of the day, commas, least em-phatic sign of recognition and difference. I have not learned to enjoy public holidays, mainly because in Dublin as a stu-dent I was far more comfortable, and more contentedly oc-cupied, in the National Library than anywhere else. My lodgings were, in one degree or another, sordid. I escaped from them either to University College or to the National Library: a desk, green-shaded light, and plenty of books. If the library was closed, as on public holidays, I had no con-genial place to go. I did not feel that festivities were designed for me. In Warrenpoint a Sunday stroll along the promenade was an agreeable diversion, but not endless in that character. Besides, I felt myself a native of the place and the Sunday visitors a nuisance: lollipops, ice cream, hubbub. A boat would have made a difference, but we did not own one. Gerard Heatley had a small one, the *Marie No. 9,* so an occasional outing was provided. Time passed, which, as Beckett says, would have passed anyway.

BRECHT SAID, according to Walter Benjamin: "Don't build on the good old days, but on the bad new ones."

KAFKA TO HIS FATHER: "I should have been happy to have you as a friend, as a chief, an uncle, a grandfather, even indeed (though this rather more hesitantly) as a father-in-law. Only as what you are, a father, you have been too strong for me, particularly since my brothers died when they were small and my sisters only came along much later, so that I had to bear the whole brunt of it all alone, something I was too weak for."* Later, Kafka speaks of his father as a figure stretched diagonally across a map of the whole world, such that he—the son—could not move a step without encountering him. I know the feeling but only by imagining it, not by having experienced it. My brother Tim probably felt that our father took up all the space of the world, but I didn't feel this. Nor could I have wanted my father to be in some

*Franz Kafka, "Wedding Preparations in the Country," in *Dearest Father: Stories and Other Writings,* tr. Ernst Kaiser and Eithne Wilkins (London: Secker and Warburg, 1954), p. 159.

other relation to me. He was born to be a father; by that I don't mean that he was the best or the most successful of fathers or the easiest in that capacity. If, thinking of Kafka's sentences, I imagine my father being not that but a friend of mine, the vision is disturbing; he would have intruded upon my life, claiming intimacies I had no inclination to offer. As my father, he occupied every space except the private one; he left me free in that quarter. We were not intimate; we had no secrets from the rest of the family. The postcards he wrote to me when I was in Tullow, regularly, every summer sound as if we were intimate, but this impression is misleading. Could it be that he found it easier to be intimate in a form which was doubly public, written rather than spoken and an open postcard rather than a letter?

YOU SHOULD NEVER get your feet wet. It rained a good deal in Warrenpoint, and without much warning, so we were often caught ill-prepared. My father did not bother to develop a theory to support his conviction that wet feet were a menace. It didn't matter if you were drenched, caught in a downpour, so long as your shoes kept you dry. He preferred boots and always wore them with his uniform, but I wanted shoes. Provided the soles were leather, he conceded the issue. But if my shoes and socks seemed wet, he insisted on my removing them and filling a tin bath with boiling water. If I soaked my feet in the bath, my father was satisfied that I might escape without damage.

Another danger to be avoided was a draught. If a window was open, the door must be closed, else a lethal draught would develop. Except for wet feet, there was nothing as bad as a draught. When a window had to be opened, my father told me to sit in the safe corner of the room, far out of harm's way. In the event, the most vulnerable part of my body turned out to be my chest, but my father seemed to think, till I got sick, that the chest could be left to look after itself. Mind your back, you're in a draught.

I HAVE TRIED to recall my father's conversation, but little of it survives, and I conclude that there was never much of it. Speech was not his medium. His silence was not gruff or nasty: it did not betoken a scene. Indeed, I surmise that most of his expressiveness was physical; it took the form of his dress, the precision of his shave, the way he walked; that, above all. Elias Canetti says, in *Crowds and Power,* that the power of remaining silent is always highly valued because it denotes the ability "to resist the innumerable provocations to speech, treating questions as though they had not been put and never letting it be seen whether what others say has caused pleasure or the reverse." The stoic virtue of imperturbability, carried to an extreme, leads to silence:

> The man who maintains a deliberate silence knows exactly what should be left unspoken. Since, in practice, no one can remain silent forever, he has to decide what can be said and what cannot. The latter is what he really knows. It is more precise and also more precious. Silence not only guards it, but gives it greater concentration. He is forced to think about it every time he has to protect it. A man who says

very little in any case always appears more concentrated than others; his silence leads one to suppose that he has much to conceal, that he is thinking of something secret.*

No, the last part is wrong; or at least it does not justly describe my father, a man of another silence. My father gave me an impression of concentration; I never saw him loose or wayward, but he implied that whatever had to be said was already said, already embodied in its entirely sufficient forms: law, custom, the daily routine. He lived as if speech were rationed and you had to save up coupons for it: there was no place for extravagance. If a new situation arose, requiring comment, one was free to speak, but sparingly. As wartime posters noted: careless talk costs lives.

Master Denis Donoghue,
Bridge Street,
Tullow,
Co. Carlow.

31st. July 1933.

Dear Denny:

I hope you are well. I am sending a view of Warrenpoint. I will be down to see you next week. Be sure you don't eat sweets, and be a good lad. I am very lonely for you. Don't let Tim go near the bridge. Are they good to you in Tullow? I was up the Bridle Lone today. From Daddy.

*Elias Canetti, *Crowds and Power,* tr. Carol Stewart (Harmondsworth, Eng.: Penguin Books, rev. ed., 1973), pp. 342–43.

Master Denis Donoghue,
Bridge Street,
Tullow,
Co. Carlow.

Wednesday, 28th. July 1937.

Dear Denis:

I hope you are not too lonely, and that you are enjoying
yourself. I trust all the others are well. I am going on well
but lonely. I hope Mrs. Dowling is better. I will see you in
a few weeks. From Daddy.

I WAS OFTEN ILL: nothing serious till the illness of my
last year at school; colds and coughs, mainly. I was put to
bed, and my mother came into the bedroom and rubbed Vick
on my chest. It had, so far as I recall, no healing power, but
the smell of Vick has remained one of my cherished memories. The rough cloth of my pyjamas is mixed in my memory
with the feeling of the buttons as I buttoned up the pyjamas
with the Vick still wet and sticky on my chest. I shared a bed
with Tim, and the mattress was so worn that there was a
valley in the middle of it, and one of us, usually Tim because
he was the elder, occupied the valley, and the other did the
best he could with the slope. The mattress was filled with
horsehair and leaked at several points. It smelled of urine. To

get from the domestic part of the house to my father's office, it was necessary to go through our bedroom. The door between the bedroom and the barracks was normally kept locked, and we were forbidden to go through except to tell my father that his dinner was ready. Late at night he sometimes went to his office or came back from it, and woke me up as he unlocked the door and came through the bedroom. Even though I knew, on each occasion, that it must be my father who was turning the key in the lock so late at night, I kept thinking that it wasn't he but was some intruder who had captured the barracks and was now going further, attacking the sergeant and his wife and children. Then I opened my eyes and saw the dark shadow walking beside the bed and crossing the landing to my parents' bedroom. In a few minutes I heard the familiar noise of my father undressing, dropping his boots on the linoleum floor.

WE WERE A CATHOLIC FAMILY. That meant that we bought our groceries at Catholic shops—Curran's, mostly, and the butcher, Fitzpatrick—and were on speaking terms only with Catholics. My mother was an exception: she was friends with Mrs. Harper, wife of one of the policemen, a Protestant. They lived in Slieve Foy Place.

Many years later, I took part in a television programme, William F. Buckley, Jr.'s *Firing Line,* debating the question of Northern Ireland with Captain Terence O'Neill, who had been Prime Minister of that dismal province. I shocked him by recalling that when I was growing up in Warrenpoint, I could spot a Protestant at a hundred yards. He claimed that this gave a most misleading impression of life in the North.

Had he not invited to tea the Prime Minister of Ireland, Sean Lemass, and was not Mr. Lemass a Catholic, and were they not the best of friends? Captain O'Neill didn't challenge me to say how I would spot a Protestant. What could I have said? I can spot a Protestant in the North of Ireland but not in the South? In the North a Protestant walks with an air of possession and authority, regardless of his social class. He walks as if he owned the place, which indeed he does. A Catholic walks as if he were there on sufferance. O'Neill is a Catholic name. How it settled upon Captain Terence or his father or grandfather, I have no idea. But if I saw him walking along Royal Avenue in Belfast and didn't know him from Adam, I would know that he was a Protestant.

The population of Warrenpoint was about two thousand in my time: a thousand Catholics, a thousand Protestants. There was no enmity between them; it was necessary only to keep your distance. My father, not given to phrasemaking, told me once that my dealings with other people should be "civil, but strange." Power, such as it was, was in the hands of the Protestants: that was all a Catholic needed to know. My father, a splendid policeman, could not be promoted: he was not a Protestant, therefore he was not a Unionist, therefore he was not a member of the Loyal Order of Orangemen, therefore . . .

THE ABILITY TO TELL a Protestant from a Catholic, in Warrenpoint, is not a skill I'm proud of, but it was a social necessity in those years. Necessary more than ever now. It was prudent to look at a man or woman, boy or girl, before leaping to the notion that you could speak. Names were a help but were not decisive. Dr. O'Tierney was a Catholic, Dr. Glenny a Protestant. Newell and Chew were Protestant names, O'Neill—the family owned the Crown Hotel, now long gone, bombed—a Catholic name. But the telling detail was the first, or Christian, name. Isabel, as I knew to my cost and pain, was a Protestant name. Denis, Timothy, Kathleen, and Mary couldn't be anything but Catholic. Patrick was an awkward case, because at a certain level of social standing and grandeur, it was a common name among Protestants. At a lower level, it was standard Catholic. In "Whatever You Say Say Nothing" Seamus Heaney writes of Northern reticence and of the

> *Manoeuvrings to find out name and school,*
> *Subtle discrimination by addresses*
> *With hardly an exception to the rule*
>
> *That Norman, Ken and Sidney signalled Prod*
> *And Seamus (call me Sean) was sure-fire Pape.**

Sometimes, and especially now, it is necessary to hear the full name before deciding where you stand. Murphy is generally a Catholic surname, but not always. The leader of the infamous Shankill Butchers was a man called Murphy, and he spent his time kidnapping and torturing Catholics. His inventiveness in that occupation was extraordinary; it is fully documented in Martin Dillon's *The Shankill Butchers: A Case Study of Mass Murder* (1989). His full name was Lennie Murphy, and anyone in Belfast could tell you that Leonard is a Protestant name. You have to learn such things, watch for signals, in Heaney's "land of password, handgrip, wink and nod."

---

*Seamus Heaney, *North* (London: Faber and Faber, 1975), p. 59.

THE PENNY CATECHISM disposed of every ethical issue in questions and answers. Question: Who is my neighbour? Answer: My neighbour is all mankind and without any exception of persons, even those who injure us or differ from us in religion.

Where, I neglected to ask, did that put Protestants?

IN WINTER, when the tide was high and the waves broke over the road between Warrenpoint and Rostrevor at Sea View Terrace, it was possible to catch fish by shooting them. Possible and illegal. You stood on the wall and waited for the precise moment when a mullet swam up to the surface between two waves, and with a "point 22" rifle you shot it. If his body turned over and you saw the white of his belly, you waded out to retrieve it. Gerard Heatley owned the rifle and let me use it now and again. Why did I want to shoot a mullet or anything else?

A strange phrase: to kill a fish. I assumed that one caught a fish or, as in this case, shot it. But many years later, when I was in Sligo to give a lecture at the Yeats Summer School, I was silently corrected in a matter of usage by T. R. Henn, Anglo-Irish Protestant scholar who spent his childhood in a manor house called Paradise. Henn mentioned that, after the school was over, he was going fishing. "Will you catch salmon or what?" I asked him. "I hope to kill salmon," the author of *The Lonely Tower: Studies in the Poetry of W. B. Yeats* answered. A Catholic wouldn't be expected to know the right word. Henn was a decent man, a good scholar, and an hospitable Fellow of St. Catherine's College, Cambridge. He was responsible for inviting me to Cambridge to give the Judith E. Wilson Lecture in Poetry and Drama, and then to take a permanent job, a university lectureship, in the English Faculty. He evidently approved of me and didn't hold my origin or my upbringing against my record. But when it came to the propriety of a verb, as a sign of one's social bearing among words, he was implacable. His voice was imperious, a bass-baritone of notable power. He once told me that in the war he had addressed a corps of troops in the desert without aid of a microphone. He recited Yeats's lyrics in the same voice, his head turned in the old lecture room in Sligo to look out upon Ben Bulben. His command of the poem was not textually perfect, he made little errors, got a word wrong here and there. But he gave the impression that accuracy didn't matter; the point was his sense of the culture he shared with Yeats. When Henn spoke of the Big House, he gave his audience to understand that his experience of that institution was at once personal and historical. One kills a salmon.

I WAS AN ALTAR BOY for a few years in the local St. Peter's Church, serving at Mass and Benediction. There were six of us. Each of us wore a black soutane and a white surplice. The surplice was stiff with starch, and my aunt Ciss made for its adornment a lace fringe embroidered with crucifixes and chalices. It was my job to ring the gong at appropriate moments during Mass. I experimented on the best sound: there was a point on the side of the gong which seemed to produce the richest sound when struck with the padded gong stick. Decorum required that the sound should not be too loud or retained too long: at the due moment, I stilled the sound by clasping the side of the gong with my hand. The responses at Mass were in Latin. *Introibo ad altare Dei,* the priest said as he mounted the four steps to the altar; and we replied, *Ad Deum qui laetificat juventutem meam.* There is no ready translation for *laetificat*: "gives joy to" is close, but it doesn't sound right. To God who gives joy to my youth. There ought to be a verb in the vicinity of joy, but the common ones are already in use for a different meaning. To God who enjoys my youth. No, that's wrong.

At Benediction of the Blessed Sacrament, the priest wore far more elaborate vestments than at Mass, and I prepared the incense and the thurible. Circular pieces of charcoal had to be placed, with some delicacy, in the bowl of the thurible and lighted. The priest, blessing the congregation, put a spoonful of incense upon the glowing charcoal, and the fumes and the smell spread throughout the chapel. You had to have the charcoal properly glowing, else the incense didn't burn properly, and the fumes were meagre. But if the charcoal burned too brightly, the incense hissed in an unmannerly fashion. "Sweet Heart of Jesus, fount of love and mercy. Today we come, Thy blessings to implore. O touch our hearts, so cold and so ungrateful. And make them, Lord, thine own for ever more." The service of Benediction ended with "Sweet Sacrament Divine: hid in Thine earthly home. Where restless yearnings cease, and sorrows all depart. Sweet Heart of Jesus, we Thee implore. O make us love Thee more and more."

I enjoyed being an altar boy at Benediction more than at Mass: it was a more colourful, more exotic event. But I knew that it was not an essential rite. You were not required to go to Benediction: it was not even a sacrament.

At school we were taught that a sacrament differed from other rites and pious practices by being a specific channel through which divine grace was imparted and received. The obligation of attending Mass every Sunday was explained and justified by that consideration. In the Catholic faith there were seven sacraments: Baptism, Confirmation, Eucharist, Penance, Extreme Unction, Holy Orders, and Matrimony. The fundamental difference between Catholicism and Protestantism was that Protestants regarded only two of these as sacraments: Baptism and Eucharist. A further difference was the refusal of Protestants to recognise His Holiness the Pope as Bishop of Rome and head of the entire Church. It followed that Protestants did not accept the teaching of the Roman Catholic Church on matters of faith and morals: most particularly, Protestants did not believe that the Pope, on the rare occasions on which he spoke *ex cathedra* and proclaimed a dogma of the Church, was infallible in doing so. On those occasions the Church could not err from the path of revealed truth.

The pious practices most frequent in Warrenpoint were these: morning and evening prayers, the family Rosary, Stations of the Cross, attending Mass on the first Friday of every month, going to church for the forty hours adoration, and taking part in the annual mission. None of these was obligatory. In Tullow Aunt Ciss was devout and insisted on the Rosary. Since the latticework of crucifixes on my surplice was her doing, I felt obliged to join her on my knees in the evening. In Warrenpoint my father and mother were less devout. My father was often out on duty, so he could not be expected to take part in the Rosary. After a few years my mother quietly gave up the attempt to convene us. It was understood that we would say our morning and night prayers, but even that was left to our private inclination. My mother did not inquire.

WHEN I SAY that I kept my distance from Protestants, I mean to say further that I did this upon instinct. But that only means I can't otherwise account for it: it was not inculcated by my parents, whom I never heard speak a word on the subject. It was simply a fact that Catholics and Protestants were different: how it became a fact is another matter. The short answer is that even if the Protestants were in the North since the Plantation of Ulster in the seventeenth century, the Catholics had to be displaced and otherwise persecuted to make room for the new arrivals. It's much like the displacement of Palestinians to make room for the Jews; except that the Jews were given the run of the whole place, and the Protestants had only a few northerly counties. Foreigners ask in dismay: How can Catholics and Protestants be killing one another, since they're all supposed to be Christians? Not a telling point; there is often the most acute enmity between people who are similar but not the same. Among the various sects of Christianity, there is more tension between Roman Catholics and High Anglicans, even though their beliefs and practices are closer than in the other, "lower" sects. The reason is that I resent someone who should be the same as me but isn't. I don't resent someone whose beliefs, technically Christian, are at the other end of the scale. Unitarians are so "low church" that they don't trouble me: I only wonder what their beliefs amount to and why they call themselves Christians. The scandal between Roman Catholics and Anglo-Catholics is that they can appear to be so close while the differences between them make it dreadful that they're not the same. It is the distance between Rome and Canterbury, between His Holiness the Pope and the Queen of England.

The movement of ecumenism in the Christian Church hasn't gone far because the points on which the participants differ are the crucial ones; the points on which they agree are superficial. My father's formula—civil but strange—was supposed to apply to everyone. There was family. And there were other people. But its bearing upon Protestants seemed to me irresistible.

CHARLOTTE STREET, then the Square, then Church Street and the park, an elegant place of grass and flowers and tennis courts and the bandstand where we had the amusements during high summer; but even before the pierrots came, you could watch the girls playing tennis, their legs and thighs white after the winter, their hair tied with a ribbon at the neck to maintain the pretence that flowing curls would impede their skill. I did not have a pair of shorts or rubber-soled shoes, so I did not play. Besides, I was a watcher: it was best to stay at a distance and live an internal life with impunity. One day, when I was watching the white-clad girls, a priest came along and sat beside me on the park bench. He was not a working priest, I knew that: he was not attached to our parish. I had seen him now and again walking along the road to Rostrevor, so I assumed that he was a patient in Mount St. Colum, as we called it, a retreat house or rest home on the shore road. He had white hair and long fingers. He started talking to me about God and the religious life. He gave me, as a gift, a copy of *The Imitation of Christ,* a leather-bound book printed on tissue paper and small enough to be concealed in the palm of my hand; a pocket book for the devout. He urged me to read a chapter of it every morning after my prayers and to think about the chapter during the day. I recall only two fragments of it. "Incline my heart to the words of thy mouth: let thy speech distill as the dew." "I will confess against myself mine own unrighteousness; I will confess my weakness unto Thee, O Lord." I promised the priest that I would always keep the book close to me and read it, but when I went home and told my father about the gift, he said it would be better to have nothing to do with a strange priest; you never knew what kind of person ended his days in Mount St. Colum.

I didn't understand the objection, though I acted upon it to the letter and avoided the priest. Years later, I came upon a similar objection in "The Sisters," one of the childhood stories in Joyce's *Dubliners*. The boy who tells the story was befriended by Father Flynn. When the priest dies, the boy's uncle says to the neighbour, old Cotter:

—The youngster and he were great friends. The old chap taught him a great deal, mind you; and they say he had a great wish for him.

Old Cotter isn't impressed:

—I wouldn't like children of mine, he said, to have too much to say to a man like that.

—How do you mean, Mr Cotter? asked my aunt.

—What I mean is, said old Cotter, it's bad for children. My idea is: let a young lad run about and play with young lads of his own age and not be . . . Am I right, Jack?

—That's my principle, too, said my uncle.*

*James Joyce, *Dubliners* (New York: Viking Compass ed., 1968), pp. 10-11.

My father did not resemble old Cotter in any other respect, but he disapproved of friendship between me and the priest. There was no good reason why a priest should enter into conversation with a boy; least of all a priest not of the parish, a man in some way mysterious or otherwise questionable. The local priests, too, should be kept at a distance. One of them, Father McMullan, was on familiar terms with the Crawford family and dropped in to Innisaimer several times a week for tea and a chat. My father thought this a regrettable matter. The Crawfords should be more careful and should not encourage informal relations between children and a priest.

THEN OR LATER, my uncle, Seamus O'Neill, gave or lent me books from a series called *Essays in Order,* published by the English Catholic publisher Sheed and Ward. The first, as I recall, was Mauriac's *God and Mammon.* From that or from some other book in the series, I committed easily to memory a sentence that stirred me to even more fervour than I already felt: "Everyone awaits the hour when he will see, not the expected face on the web of his past, but the face of his Maker, agonisingly sweet and covered with blood." I recited the phrases, sometimes in the sequence of the sentence, sometimes detached from it: agonisingly sweet, everyone awaits the hour, covered with blood, the face of his Maker. Bernanos's *Diary of a Country Priest* was another gift from my pious uncle. The image of sanctity which it fixed in my mind was, I now see, too French to be sought; unlike Mauriac's, which I didn't see as French but as universal. "First you must kneel," the *curé* demands of Chantal when she brings to him in the church her jealousy and hatred. Later, to her mother, the *Comtesse,* he says—I have never forgotten the admonition—"God is not to be bargained with. We must give ourselves up to Him unconditionally. There are not two kingdoms, one for the living, one for the dead."

I have never understood why people hate Christianity, especially people who express shock at the least trace of anti-Semitism. Why are Jews supposed to be cared for but not Christians? Is it because of the Holocaust, and despite the fact that Jews in Israel have shown themselves just as merciless as Arabs or Germans or Japanese or Irishmen or anyone else? Or because there are more Christians in the world than Jews? I could never understand how William Empson, a poet and critic I revere, could hate Christians and especially Catholics, thinking their religion nothing but a sordid cult of blood and sacrifice. Christ's blood was the form of his own suffering, he didn't recommend bloodletting for other people. Empson thought that Christians, because of the Crucifixion, are besotted with pain and suffering, the Agony in the Garden their favourite emotion. On the contrary, the founding event in Christianity is the Incarnation, when God in the form of the Christ-child came into time and history, with the hope and offer of redemption. Yeats said that "twenty centuries of stony sleep / Were vexed to nightmare by a rocking cradle," and he thought that the next twenty would be dominated by a different force, some rough beast slouching towards Bethlehem. But he didn't blame Christians, as Empson did, for every drop of blood shed in just or unjust cause.

THE CATECHISM was not especially informative about God. Who is God? God is the Creator and King, Lord and Owner of Heaven and Earth and of all things. Not that I needed to be informed. God was not a problem unless one insisted on characterising Him. Then the meagreness of one's vocabulary made the effort seem vain. Why should God be amenable to the grammar and diction of the English language? If the matter in hand was one's feeling about God, then there was no great problem; it became an occasion of subjective description. It seems pointless to leap from "how I feel about God" to "who or what God is."

I didn't pester myself with such questions, but I remember adverting to them. Sitting one day, "drowsing in sunlight," on the Crawfords' seat, I had the only metaphysical thought that ever occurred to me, a version, as I later discovered, of a famous meditation in Leibniz. In *Principles of Nature and Grace,* Leibniz asks himself: Why is there something rather than nothing? I do not recall asking myself that precise question, but rather another one, which turns out also to have been asked by Leibniz: Why are there these things rather than other things that might be imagined?* Leibniz argues that there is reason in nature why something should exist rather than nothing, as a consequence of the principle that nothing

---

*Leibniz, *Principes de la nature et de la grace, fondés en raison*: ". . . la premiere question qu'on a droit de faire, sera, Pourquoy il y plustôt quelque chose que rien? Car le rien est plus simple et plus facile que quelque chose. De plus, supposé que des choses doivent exister, il faut qu'on puisse rendre raison, pourquoy elles doivent existent ainsi, et non autrement." *Die Philosophischen Schriften von Gottfried Wilhelm Leibniz,* ed. G. J. Gerhardt, 7 vols., 1875–90 (Hildesheim: Ohms, 1978), p. 602.

happens without a reason. And also because there must be a reason—my question, regrettably anticipated—why this thing exists rather than another. "In all essence," according to Leibniz, "there is a striving for existence." Presumably this striving, in many hypothetical cases, fails. It is possible to imagine things that don't exist: a violin-playing mermaid, a flute-playing centaur. Not that I can see the point of positing an essence such that, if it were to strive successfully for existence, it would take the form of that mermaid or that centaur. But the fact that something exists rather than nothing continues to appear significant. Significant of what? The self-evident existence of the world or of anything (including the mind or whatever-it-is that frames the sentence) seemed to me to presuppose One who created it. I couldn't take seriously the notion that it came into being by chance. "We live in an old chaos of the sun": very likely. But that doesn't strengthen any prejudice in favour of chance rather than design. If by chance, there was nothing to be said. If by design, then the word "God" was as good a name as any the English language could produce.

The existence of God wasn't a particular problem for me. It could be that "existence" was not necessarily the right word: it might be the case that to posit a divine power as existing was merely a congenial way of expressing one's desire that it should be so. But the ascription of further human qualities to God seemed to me exorbitant. I couldn't see any reason why God should resemble me. I could see that if God was the Lord of all, one would say such a thing only because my father was, in his constricted circumstances, the lord of a little all. But the argument from analogy was useless. I was content to let the difference between God and Man remain absolute and to regard Christ as a sufficient body of mediation. One could delineate Christ well enough, as the priests did. There was no need to delineate God. Any attempt to do so seemed to me blasphemous, a flagrant essay in domestication. If the difference between God and Man is absolute, there is no merit in nagging the subject or haggling with God, dragging Him before the tribunal of a purely human justice. Why, if God is omnipotent, does He allow evil to persist and thrive in the world? The question didn't seem to me to arise. I could not see any reason why God should accept our terms of judgment or be accounted innocent or guilty in our eyes.

IN OUR HOUSE, religion was practised but not discussed. We were reared as Catholics, but the tenets of our Catholicism were not issues to be engaged or defined. Frequent reception of the sacraments was required: that is, we went to confession on Saturday night so that we could duly receive Holy Communion at Mass on Sunday. I always went to Father McMullan's confession box because he was known to be friendly. The problem was to find anything worth confessing. I had only the vaguest notion of a sin and rarely recognised my conduct as falling into that category. It was not feasible to kneel down in the darkness of the confession box and claim that I had not committed any sins since my last good confession. So I invented a few: "It is a week since my last good confession, Father. In that time I have told two lies, said three bad words. That's all, Father." It did not strike me as reprehensible that in confessing to two lies I told the only lie of my week. The bad words were sinful enough, so the addition of two lies I hadn't told made up a decent sum. Father McMullan admonished me to stop telling lies and to watch out for the bad words because they formed a bad habit of speech. Then he gave me the penance: three Hail Marys and an Act of Contrition. As I got to my feet to leave, he said: "Will Tim be all right for tomorrow?" He meant: "Will Tim's injury be healed up in time to play for the Warrenpoint Gaelic Football Club's match with Mayobridge?"

It was hard to feel contrite. I knelt down, put my head in my hands for secrecy and concentration, talked myself into remorse. But the sins, even the genuine ones, seemed meagre incitements to contrition.

It did not strike me that telling a lie in confession was a dreadful thing to do. It constituted a sacrilege, and I knew what a sacrilege was; it entailed desecrating a sacrament, as if one spat out the sacred Host upon receiving it in Holy Communion. I suppose that what seemed most important, for domestic reasons, was the practice of going to confession. What one confessed was a matter of moment, but if I had nothing to confess, I could hardly go to confession and waste the priest's time. Only three sins were known to me: telling lies, saying bad words, and having impure thoughts. I never had impure thoughts. The questionable words I said were few and rough rather than bad, minor obscenities at worst. That left lies, a matter more complex than I thought it to be. Whenever I told a lie, I told it to escape punishment or domestic strife. If I said something that was not true, I took it for granted that it was a lie. I didn't know the difference, which Rousseau goes to some length in the fourth *Rêverie* to establish, between a lie and a fiction. A lie, if you believe Rousseau, is an untruth told to avoid some embarrassment, unpleasantness, or punishment, or to inflict hurt upon someone. A fiction is something one makes up which is entirely innocuous in that respect. Anything that, contrary to truth, does not interest justice in any way, according to Rousseau, is nothing but a fiction, "and I declare that whoever reproaches himself for a pure fiction as a deceit has a more delicate conscience than I have." I don't think this criterion is valid. The question of justice is momentous, but it is not the sole consideration. When I told Father McMullan in confession that I had told two lies—why two, by the way, since one would have been enough to give him something to absolve?—I didn't commit an injustice against anyone. The matter, so far as consequences were in question, was indifferent. The fault, as it now appears, is that I had made light of the sacrament; I had "made a mockery," as my mother used to say in another regard, of a sacred thing; it was like smashing a monstrance.

The penny Catechism did not run to Rousseau's equivocations: it declared that "no lie can be lawful or innocent; no motive, however good, can excuse a lie, because a lie is always sinful and bad in itself." That sentence was my first encounter with the intellectual or moral idea of the intrinsic.

At school in Warrenpoint, we learned the truths of the Catholic faith mainly by memorising the penny Catechism, a set of doctrines and dogmas of the Church. A year or two later, still in Warrenpoint, we read a larger Catechism, which proceeded by question-and-answer. The questions were not always obvious; they would not have struck me as requiring to be formulated. But the answers were satisfactorily decisive. At the Christian Brothers' we studied a book called *Apologetics and Catholic Doctrine*, largely based upon the papal encyclicals and a commentary on each. The matters contained in these books were not texts for discussion or debate: they were to be received, committed to memory, not debated or haggled over.

I can't recall how I received these doctrines and dogmas. It was not a case of approving or disapproving, any more than the character of the Latin subjunctive called for debate. The dogmatic character of the Church was what most fully satisfied me. I wanted to belong to a church that knew its mind because it had received that knowledge from God by way of scripture and tradition. I assumed that the dogmatism of the Church was innate in its character. In fact it isn't. I gather from Hans Blumenberg's *The Legitimacy of the Modern Age* that it was only in response to the dangerous theodicy of Gnosticism, and in particular to its most formidable spokesman, Marcion, that the Church was forced, "in the interest of consolidation, to define itself in terms of dogma." Blumenberg argues that "the formation of the Middle Ages can only be understood as an attempt at the definitive exclusion of the Gnostic syndrome." To retrieve the world as the creation "from the negative role assigned to it by the doctrine of its demiurgic origin, and to salvage the dignity of the ancient cosmos for its role in the Christian system, was the central effort all the way from Augustine to the height of Scholasticism."*

This effort explains, too, the other great dogma which I received in the Christian Brothers' without much fuss, the doctrine of Original Sin. Even after Augustine had given up his Manichaean affiliation, he had to account for the evil forces in a world apparently the creation of an omnipotent and just God. The only way he could think of explaining these was by attributing to man every evil in the world, and deeming them to be the just punishment imposed by a just God for man's sins. The problem was that, as Blumenberg says, in order to deserve as punishment the evil world as it had been perceived and adjudged by the Manichaeans, the sins of man, "which take over the position of the wickedness of the Gnostic

*Hans Blumenberg, *The Legitimacy of the Modern Age,* tr. Robert M. Wallace (Cambridge, Mass.: MIT Press, 1983), pp. 126ff.

demiurge, had to be great." Augustine wrote the *Confessions* partly to see whether he could find in his own actions any evil commensurate with the scale of punishment represented by the evil of the world. He could not find anything bad enough. So he had to posit a mythic or aboriginal sin great enough to explain the punishment meted out by God. "The balance," as Blumenberg says, "between the condition of the world and the guilt of mankind, which Augustine had drawn up in his early philosophy of freedom, caused him to become the theologian of the uniquely great original guilt of mankind and of its mythical inheritance." The doctrine of divine grace, "a supernatural gift bestowed upon us by God for our salvation," as the Catechism said, was understandable in these terms. Salvation must be possible, since God sent his beloved Son to offer it to men free to choose: grace was the form of the offer.

In the practice of autobiography the main difference between Augustine and Rousseau is that for Augustine, the final judge is God, the Last Judgment is irrevocable; for Rousseau, he himself is the judge, the Last Judgment is his writing of the *Confessions,* and what passes for grace is the shamelessness with which he tells the shoddy as well as the heroic truth about himself. Autobiography becomes an interior court, the writer is at once criminal and judge, and the only law is the one that requires total disclosure. The fact that Rousseau returned to the courtroom, in the *Rêveries,* and wrote a different speech for himself is interesting but irrelevant.

The doctrine of Original Sin gave me no special difficulty. I did not feel inclined to ask: What exactly did Adam and Eve do that was so terrible? Was their disobedience unpardonable? It didn't occur to me as a problem that the entire human race was in some sense guilt-ridden: if we clearly weren't angels, we did not seem plausible as devils. Only in later years did a problem arise, and even then I could see that it wasn't the same problem. It was common, especially when Hannah Arendt published *Eichmann in Jerusalem,* to talk of modern guilt as if we were all deemed to share it. I could neither feel guilty about the Final Solution nor see the merit of working myself into a frenzy over a sin I demonstrably hadn't committed. I had no difficulty in distinguishing, as a Catholic, between Original Sin and specific sin: the one was categorical, a state of being, inherent in human life as such, a mythic state embodied in the narrative of Adam and Eve but a state which otherwise was under no obligation to be historical; the other was a particular sinful act, my responsibility, which I could deal with only by repentance, confession, and the receipt of absolution. The problem with the imputed guilt of the Holocaust is that it is clearly historical, like my particular sins, but I could not believe that the two "sins" were committed in history, least of all in recent history, and had similar historical provenance.

IN *Aids to Reflection* COLERIDGE has a testy comment on Original Sin. "If it be Sin," he argued, "it must be *original,*" so the phrase is tautology. "A State or Act, that has not its origin in the will, may be calamity, deformity, disease, or mischief; but a *Sin* it cannot be." The speed with which he gathers together "a State or Act," as if they were synonymous, makes me pause. If it has not its origin in the will, it is not an act, but it may be a state. The doctrine of Original Sin is clear regardless of whether we observe it: it refers to a state of guilt which we inherit from our First Parents, who committed an actual sin of disobedience against God. The guilt is categorical, in the sense that it devolves upon each of us;

by virtue of being human, we inherit it as a mark or shadow upon our souls. Coleridge refuses to distinguish between Original Sin and actual sin: he treats Original Sin as if it were actual sin and then declares it no sin at all because it has not its origin in the will.

The doctrine has never seemed harsh or even illogical to me. As a child, I felt myself always in the vicinity of guilt, even though there was no sin of which I could accuse myself. I did not think it unjust that I should have come into the world at a late moment in human history or that I should in some sense inherit an aboriginal state of guilt. The state sustained itself not upon prophecies of Hell-fire and damnation—I never heard a sermon like the one in *A Portrait of the Artist as a Young Man;* nor, indeed, did Joyce—but upon a sense, more or less acute, of belatedness. I had indeed come late into the world; it was vain to think that my soul should be without shadow.

I had no difficulty, then, with the doctrine of Original Sin. My body was sufficient evidence for it. I saw no discrepancy between the ungainliness of my body and the supposition that the human body as such came already corrupted into a world disfigured by its presence. That there were beautiful bodies in the same world seemed to me not to incapacitate the doctrine but to intimate the presence of divine grace. Isabel Bridges was the visible sign of one, as I of the other. That a certain few people were saints or geniuses held out the possibility of salvation, but it didn't remove my conviction that to be a body was to be constitutionally and categorically polluted. The question was: How to act in the light or the shadow of that fate? My father's way of being in the world seemed to me to offer the best hope of salvation.

In school Original Sin was explained as a fundamental act of transgression, an act of disobedience committed by our First Parents, but chiefly by Adam. It was an act of will, Adam's willing refusal of the divine commandment. The woman tempted me and I did eat: a wretched excuse. Adam ate of the tree of knowledge, disobeying the command of God, which had every right to be arbitrary. I remember wondering: Why did God impose His law upon Adam, knowing that he would break it? Admittedly, God left Adam free to obey Him or not, but He must have known, since He knows all things, that Adam would be wilful enough to disobey Him. I was not shocked by this reasoning: the responsibility still rested upon Adam.

It never occurred to me that the transgression was a sexual act rather than an act of disobedience. My body was burdensome but not because of sexual impulses or desires: it was too big, a poor receptacle for whatever spiritual stirrings I had; but it did not occur to me to regard its sexual character as crucial. When I came upon the Pauline and Augustinian interpretation of Original Sin as fleshly, I was shocked, but I didn't believe it. The sequence by which the serpent tempted Eve, who in turn tempted Adam, seemed to me just as credible if the object was forbidden knowledge as if it was forbidden sexual indulgence. I could imagine primordial sin in one form just as easily as in the other, and with more point. Besides, it was Adam's sin, I believed, more than Eve's: his was the will, the determination, and therefore the responsibility.

In the same spirit, going to confession, I did not object either to the sacrament or to its official procedures: contrition, confession, satisfaction, and absolution. The form seemed satisfactory, especially as I did not feel any intellectual difficulty in the idea of the priest as minister, representative of God. The fact that the priest was also, in another respect, a mere man was irrelevant. I could see that a Mass celebrated by a priest who also happened to be a thief or an adulterer was just as valid as one celebrated by a walking saint: the sacrifice was impersonal, and sublime for that reason.

Contrition was hard, especially as I was rarely aware of

having committed a sin. Kneeling in prayer while waiting for the line of penitents to reduce itself to me—as we moved up toward the confession box, impatiently, and looked hard at any emerging sinner whose confession had taken a long time—my "examination of conscience" usually required me to enliven my general sense of heaviness and discrepancy. A sin made the process easier, but it was not really necessary. Confession was nearly automatic, the same routine of speech, week by week. Julia Kristeva has argued, in *Powers of Horror,* that "the practice of confession, upon the whole, does nothing else but weigh down discourse with sin":

> By having it bear that load, which alone grants it the inten-
> sity of full communication, avowal absolves from sin and,
> by the same stroke, founds the power of discourse.

I had always thought that confession, being a sacrament, was part of the Church since the first Peter, but evidently not: it was extended from monks to laity only in the thirteenth century, by decision of the fourth Lateran Council. Kristeva isn't concerned with that: she is dealing with "the ultimate interiorization of sin within discourses, by the final postulate that does away with an offense because of its enunciation before the One."* Her argument for this idea is that Christianity took up the abominations as specified in Leviticus but internalised them: abjection was no longer external; it was permanent and came from within. "Not that which goeth into the mouth defileth a man; but that which cometh out of the mouth, this defileth a man" (Matthew 15:11). Christ interiorised abomination as sin and offered the Christian soul the fate of being a lapsing subject or the providence of being a saved one. But—a point Kristeva ignores—in confession the

---

*Julia Kristeva, *Powers of Horror: An Essay on Abjection,* tr. Leon S. Roudiez (New York: Columbia University Press, 1982), p. 130.

mere word is not enough, the uttering of normative sounds: indeed, if the words spoken are not true, the confession is blasphemy, a return to abomination. The words spoken are the mere decorum of the spiritual act; it is the speech of the heart, the conscience, that counts, not the acoustic phenomenon. I agree with Kristeva that the purpose of confession is to weigh down discourse with sin, a peculiarly substantive act in a medium liable otherwise to be absurdly volatile.

Satisfaction: that rarely arose, but it denoted making reparation to anyone the penitent had offended. If I had stolen a pen, I would have been required to restore it to its lawful owner or otherwise make up to him for the theft. The more customary object of satisfaction was God, wounded by my sin in thought, word, or deed. Contrition and satisfaction were virtually the same. The point of satisfaction was to put the penitent's soul in good standing again, either with other souls, as in a community, or with God. Absolution ensued: a token penance unless the sin was dire. In theory one emerged from the confessional a forgiven boy, lighter, happier, now that he was reconciled to his Maker.

Communion followed at Mass the following morning. The priest's communion took place through the species of bread and wine: he broke and ate the wafer, then drank wine from a silver chalice, finally washed his hands. The congregation approached the altar and received the wafer directly into the mouth; in those days there was no manual reception of the Host. The doctrine of the Eucharist was explained, at school, by reference to Christ's miraculous feeding of the multitude with loaves and fishes, a chapter in Mark that seemed to answer any questions I felt inclined to ask.

AT MASS I HEARD things I did not understand, and devised for myself the exotic pleasure of being in their presence without comprehension. "For the children of darkness are wiser in their generation than the children of light." What could it mean, unless the Prince of Darkness was wiser, too, than the Prince of Light? Or wiser in the beginning, even if proved a fool in the end. But I wasn't worried by my failure to comprehend. I was content not to understand, so long as I was in the vicinity of the words themselves. The syntax of the sentence was assured, and I took consolation from the march of its certitude. For the children . . . It remained a dark saying, but I listened to the conviction in the words rather than to the mere meaning of the declaration. When Desdemona, protesting to Othello, says: "I understand a fury in your words, / But not the words," I take her words, the discrimination of the phrasing, as enacting a meaning prior to the declared meaning and superior to it. Pride, bewilderment, the pride of being bewildered in such a good cause: these motives seem to have inhabited the sentence a split second before the mere meaning of it identifies itself and slips out of the sentence. The children of darkness: who are they? Not, surely, mere sinners, but people who have issued from centuries of darkness and sin. Wiser: street wise, worldly wise where innocence would only be silly. In their generation: not just in their time, but in the condition of their generation, their having issued from time and flesh. It's still opaque. Why, in a church founded upon the child Christ and the innocence of little children, should the wisdom of darkness be extolled? I gave it up, but not as a conundrum which I should at some point try to solve: it did not sound like a riddle or even in need of interpretation. The lion and the honeycomb made a riddle, and it was necessary to turn it into narrative sense, a wise saw. But the wisdom of the children of darkness could be left in the dark. My spiritual life did not depend upon it.

A MILE OR THEREABOUTS out of Omeath on the Carlingford Road there was an open-air shrine popularly known as Calvary: its official name was Mount St. Carmel. There was an altar, and the field was laid out as the Stations of the Cross. At every station there was an image of the Agony, culminating in the Crucifixion. It was a standard trip to make. You could walk, if you had a mind to, or go by horse and jaunting car, a jollier method and pleasant on a sunny day. The jaunting car held four people, not counting the driver, two on either side. While the men were drinking in the public houses up from the jetty, the women and children made the little pilgrimage to Calvary. The Stations of the Cross are a rare devotion now but were common in my day: women, especially, did the stations in the few minutes before Mass. At each of the fourteen stations you recited the appropriate phrase: the first station, Jesus is condemned to death; the second station, Jesus is stripped of his garments. The first time I heard the word "afflicted" was at the stations: Jesus meets his afflicted mother. Jesus falls the first time. If a priest were conducting the service, he called out the title of the station—Veronica wipes our Lord's face—and asked the congregation to "consider" some aspect of the event. At the end of the consideration he said: "I love Thee, Jesus, my love above all things. I repent of my whole heart for having offended

Thee. Never permit me to separate myself from Thee again. Grant that I may love Thee always, and then do with me what Thou wilt." Was it the Our Father or the Hail Mary that followed, when priest and congregation knelt down? Isn't it odd that I can't remember that detail while I recall easily the ritual that preceded it? Catholic churches still have the fourteen stations on the walls, but I haven't seen anyone doing the stations for years now.

I WENT TO THE LOCAL Catholic school, St. Peter's, a building with three rooms and three teachers: Mr. Clancy, Mr. Crawford, and Miss McDonald. Mr. Clancy was the principal. Every morning, half an hour after class started, he left his room and walked down to the Liverpool Hotel, where he drank till he was well drunk, then came back to school to assault Miss McDonald. Miss McDonald, who taught the youngest children, hearing Mr. Clancy coming, jammed a wedge of wood under her door, turned the key shut, and put her shoulder to the door. Mr. Clancy crashed against the door, but, as he was drunk, his movements were sluggish, no match for a wedge, a lock, and Miss McDonald. After a joyless bout of shoving and crashing, Mr. Clancy went back to his own class, muttering under his sodden breath. He had a nervous tic. He kept twitching the point of his nose with his thumb and seemed to keep his nails long for that purpose. His room contained the chemistry laboratory, a glass case with three or four bottles of acids, a Bunsen burner, a pipette, and a scales. These were never used, except on one afternoon, while the class was on lunch break, Mr. Clancy took one of the bottles containing sulphuric acid, drank it, and killed himself. I don't remember if he was replaced, or who got the principal's job, because soon after I went to school in Newry.

My teacher at St. Peter's was Mr. Crawford, a man who lived for music and stories. When he heard Mr. Clancy leaving for the Liverpool Hotel, Mr. Crawford climbed upon a desk at the back of the room to verify Mr. Clancy's departure, and then, satisfied, settled down to tell us stories and to talk about music. He had strange hands. His nails were bitten down to the quick, and the palms of his hands were as soft as butter. He played the organ in the church, and I was in the choir. His hands were always lower than the keyboard, and his fingers seemed to climb to the notes as if slithering over a wall. When he pressed the keys, the skin of his fingers spread itself wide and flat, as if it wanted to adhere to the notes. Years later, I came across a passage in Ralph Cusack's autobiography, *Cadenza,* where he describes an old man, in a café somewhere in Provence, playing silent piano on the surface of the table and bending his head to hear the sounds. After a while Cusack discovered, by following the old man's fingers, that he was playing Beethoven's *Moonlight Sonata.* Mr. Crawford never looked at the keyboard while he was playing. His head kept darting and straining from side to side, as if the music came from some secret place and he had to find it.

He was a terrible teacher, except for stories and the talk of music. He, too, left the room as often as the coast was clear and Mr. Clancy gone, but Mr. Crawford only went for a walk. He had a peculiar manner of walking, always on the bias. If you walked along the street with him, he kept cutting across your path and crowding you off the pavement, as if he hated a straight line. His body was in some acute or oblique relation to his soul. Even if he intended to walk from his house at the west corner of the square to go up Church Street, he always left the pavement and walked as if he were going to the school or the church, and then he would wheel back, tacking his way till he got to where he was going. When he absented himself from the classroom, we resumed the only entertainment available. The room had a high wooden ceiling, and we wrote with Waverley pens, which had wooden stems and long, pointed steel nibs. If you flung the pen hard and true, you could get it to lodge in the ceiling. If it fell down, it had a good chance of hitting someone on the head. Either way, it was worth trying. During the school year the ceiling acquired an impressive array of Waverley pens. At the end of the year, they were removed, and we started afresh.

The guardian or administrator of the school on behalf of the church was Archdeacon McAllister, a man of notable greed. I don't recall that he ever came to the school, but every Sunday, as we went into church for Mass, the archdeacon was standing over a collection plate and observing the contributions of his flock. He also had a strange custom in regard to funerals. When someone died and the body was brought to the church for a service, the archdeacon prescribed that dues— he called them offerings—would be paid before the funeral would proceed to the cemetery. It was also customary that the highest payers would start off the proceedings, coming up to the altar and placing the money on the collection plate. To avoid any mistake, the archdeacon would call out in a loud voice the man's name and the amount of his offering. The mourners then arranged themselves accordingly, approaching the altar in descending financial order. It was not the case in Warrenpoint that the last would be first and the first last. My father created a disturbance with Archdeacon McAllister—or was he only a canon then?—by refusing to have offerings collected over the remains of an infant. I don't see the difference; it was merely a matter, on the archdeacon's part, of domestic economy, like income tax or sales tax. My conviction that he was greedy arises not from any visible extravagance on his part but from the fact that he seemed to take pleasure in financial work: he stood over the collection plate as if there more than elsewhere he was in truth doing God's work.

I HAD A GOOD boy-soprano voice. I sang solo in the choir at Mass. *O salutaris hostia. Pange lingua. Ave Maria.* Before my voice broke, my father decided to have it recorded in some form. We cycled to Dublin, where we sought out Walton's Musical Store, 90 Lower Camden Street. We had no accompanist, but it happened that a man called Chris Sylvester, who played piano and accordion in his brother Ralph's dance band, was in Walton's when we presented our case. He offered to accompany me, and we went upstairs to a room large enough to contain me but not a piano. We left the door open, and Mr. Sylvester played the piano in the next room, where the pianos were displayed for sale. A wax recording was made of my performance of "Silent Night" on one side and "Panis Angelicus" on the other. I broke down on the first attempt at "Silent Night," but the second attempt was deemed satisfactory. And it was. I was not the finest boy soprano of my time or later—that Welsh boy Aled Jones is of a different order of sweetness and range—but I was good.

Later, when I came to be a student at University College, Dublin, I combined my work in English and Latin with more enjoyable studies in *lieder*-singing and the theory of music at the Royal Irish Academy of Music. My teacher was Brian Boydell, a composer, an oboist, and a painter, the first example of an artist I ever met. We worked through Schumann's *Dichterliebe* and moved on to some Elizabethan music, Dowland mainly. I always liked to sing songs that were already poetry: Roger Quilter's setting of Tennyson's "Now Sleeps the Crimson Petal," Vaughan Williams's setting of Rossetti's "Silent Noon":

> *Your hands lie open in the long fresh grass—*
> *The finger-points look through like rosy blooms;*
> *Your eyes smile peace.*

The problem in singing songs that are already poetry is that you are inclined to caress the words rather than let them utter themselves. When I sang "Now Sleeps the Crimson Petal," I couldn't help lingering over the continuation of the line, "now the white," as if its monosyllables needed to be fondled. Boydell couldn't get me to maintain the decency of appearing to sing the words as if they hardly needed to be sung at all. I sang them as if in italics. Or if I tried to be neutral, I ended up seeming casual. Singing is difficult. I loved "Silent Noon," but it was hard to sing the second line and make it clear that "points" was the completion of a compound noun, "finger-points," not a verb issuing from "finger." As I sang the line, it sounded as if it had two strangely unrelated verbs coming after the expected noun. It was hard, in the third line, to sing "your eyes" and distinguish the words from "you rise." It could be done, but only by having an awkward gap between "your" and "eyes." When I tried to sing songs in Irish, like "Una Bhán," I couldn't keep the musical line going while attending to the ornamentation. German was easier to sing, once I had got the pronunciation right, though I found the sustained momentum of "Es ist vollbracht" a stretch. Boydell assured me that I would improve with years and development, but by then I had decided that a musical career was impossible. Besides, I had turned to literature. I continued to take part in Dublin's musical life when I left UCD and got a job as a civil servant, an administrative officer in the Department of Finance. I spent an acrimonious year as music critic for *The Irish Times,* reporting mainly on the activities of the Radio Éireann Orchestra, a fallible instrument at that time. But then I was "a young man doing his best to get on in the world," and turned my hand to several interests.

A PASSAGE FROM Susanne K. Langer's *Feeling and Form*:

> For the elements of music are not tones of such and such pitch, duration and loudness, nor chords and measured beats; they are, like all artistic elements, something virtual, created only for perception. Eduard Hanslick denoted them rightly: "tönend bewegte Formen"—"sounding forms in motion." . . . The semblance of this vital, experiential time is the primary illusion of music. All music creates an order of virtual time, in which its sonorous forms move in relation to each other—always and only to each other, for nothing else exists there. Virtual time is as separate from the sequence of actual happenings as virtual space from actual space.*

Presumably she means that virtuality, the state of an element created only for perception, differs from every other state in which that element is found, since perception is only one of many human motives or needs and is not, indeed, the most fundamental of those. But virtuality is a difficult concept. The dictionaries say that it means essential nature or being,

*Susanne K. Langer, *Feeling and Form: A Theory of Art* (London: Routledge and Kegan Paul, 1953), pp. 107, 109.

apart from external form or embodiment; or the power by which one grain of corn issues in many. But sometimes the word is used to denote potentiality, a latent capacity waiting to become actual, as Carlyle in *Past and Present* writes of "a Virtuality perfected into an Actuality." In Langer's use of the word it is necessary to hold virtuality and actuality as separate categories: one state is not superior to the other. Actuality serves many needs, virtuality only one, that of perception. Now, what follows if Langer is right?

CERTAIN QUESTIONS are adequately answered by re-marking the folly of asking them, as Augustine argued that it was trivial of the Manichees to inquire what God was doing before He created the universe. It is a false question to ask: What does a piece of music mean? Music is expressive, but on condition that it is not called upon to specify in other terms what it expresses. Suppose you are listening to Beethoven's Sonata for Piano and Violin no. 5, op. 24: the key is F major. The piece is traditionally, but for poor reason, called the *Spring*. In the first movement the instruments have been answering each other, coming together, moving apart, coming together again. But the second movement, marked *adagio molto espressivo,* begins with the piano alone, 3/4 time in B-flat, the first bar three beats of arpeggio-figure, four semi-quavers in the bass, the first and third beats identically swaying between B-flat, D, and F, the middle one rising to the B-flat an octave higher. Nothing happens in the treble until the second bar, when a held minim D, still on the piano, intro-duces the new melody: it sounds like a piano sonata, or as if the violin had departed. The violin enters, in unison with the piano's inaugural D, but on the second beat of the bar, not the first; where the piano melody starts each bar with an accented minim or dotted crotchet and leaves the arabesquing for the third beat, the violin intervenes with detached two-note phrases, marking the second and third beats of the bar, a crotchet, a quaver, a quaver rest; the next bar begins with a crotchet rest while the piano keeps the melody. The fact that the violin sketches the piano's official melody in reverse, moving down the scale, doesn't impede the privilege of the piano. It is as if the violin assented to the dominance of the piano and contented itself to annotate a far more expansive gesture than anything it would propose on its own behalf. Or as if the violin anticipated the syncopation, in bars 10 to 27 of the *scherzo* movement, again a nuance of unison rather than a breach of it. Meanwhile, violin and piano cooperate in what Schenker would call "a composing out," receiving the movement from B-flat to the higher B-flat, which the piano negotiated in the first beat of the movement, and elaborating it, the violin traversing it in five beats, the piano in six.

What these little acts suggest is that music makes sense but doesn't offer meaning. The sense it makes can't be arrived at—and is best if not pestered—by starting from certain common or unusual experiences we might have in our ordinary lives and then correlating them with episodes in a particular piece of music. It seems better to start with something like the realm of Platonic ideas, assume that they are eternally true and lack, for their perfection, only some accessible form of appearance. Stevens speaks, in "To the One of Fictive Music," of giving "motion to perfection," as if without it any perfection is imperfect or at best intolerable. We may fancy that the Platonic forms are not accessible now but that they may become accessible. But not in music. In music the ideas—call them that for the moment—never coincide so fully with a lived or living form as to give up their virtual status. The opening of the *adagio* movement in Beethoven's sonata does not offer to show what partnering is like or even what its ideal form would be. The sensuous character of the music corresponds not to the idea of partnering or even to its imputed gratifications, but to one of many formal destinies it might find for itself. "Sonata" is the name of every possible destiny available in a certain genre. Virtuality is never set aside, but the possibility of setting it aside and coming boldly into appearance is one of the feelings the music risks provoking.

No, that is not quite right. Try again. Beethoven's sonata does not enact a relation or relations such as one enjoys or fails to enjoy in ordinary life. Nothing is imitated: even in "programme music" the relation between certain sounds and certain common experiences is not accurately described as imitation. No hooves gallop in Schubert's "Erlkönig," not even mimed hooves. The sonata invokes certain experiences but holds them in a state of virtuality: we are to construe them as forms which, in performance, provoke the listener to feel; they are intimations as if prior to their perpetually postponed fall into chronological time. Mallarmé intuits such virtuality in the sixth stanza of "Prose (pour des Esseintes)":

> *Oui, dans une île que l'air charge*
> *De vue et non de visions*
> *Toute fleur s'étalait plus large*
> *Sans que nous en devisions.*

Perhaps: yes, an island which the air charges with sight and not with visions, every flower spreads itself out more grandly without our speaking of it. Stevens's version is "On the Road Home":

It was when I said,
"There is no such thing as the truth,"
That the grapes seemed fatter.

Mallarmé seems to say that nothing is privileged merely by virtue of the fact that it has come into existence, or that it is now such that we can hold it in our visions and talk about it. By coming into existence, it has gained the force of being, but at the expense of the many other forms it might have taken: virtuality is the site of those hypothetical forms; *vue* is the imaginative act which registers their possibility and stops short of prescribing any one of them. Visions are the imperious form of cognition; *vue* is the heuristic form which is content that the objects of its attention will remain indeterminate, as if attentiveness were content not to have an object. Music is the art which gives a formal destiny, in each case, to feelings which are still free to postpone their dependence upon particular objects and events: it does not summarise or generalise experiences which we might recognise in other terms—even to speak of partnering is misleading for that reason. Nor does it negotiate essences in opposition to existences, unless we think of essence as purely notional, a logic upon which the virtualities of musical forms and relations are predicated. Beethoven's sonata does not intuit the essence or the idea of partnering; it does not abstract from partnerships the qualities they have in general, such that we are justified in calling them by that name. Rather, it starts with—to repeat—an eternal idea or value and gives it the freedom of assuming qualities other than those immobilised by our recognising them. Mallarmé again: the fragrance which the idea has—or, let us say, the sonata has—is the one absent from all bouquets and from our insistent sense of them.

IN THE SIXTH book of *De Musica* Augustine speaks of the unity of water, sky, air. Then—W. J. Jackson Knight's synopsis of the treatise—he says:

> Anything which the ministry of carnal perception can count, and anything contained in it, cannot be furnished with, or possess, any numerical rhythm in space which can be estimated, unless previously a numerical rhythm in time has preceded in silent movement. Before even that, there comes vital movement, agile with temporal intervals, and it modifies what it finds, serving the Lord of All Things.

What can this movement be, if not primordial energy, the Word of God, unchanging though the cause of change? Augustine believes that poetry, even the poetry of the Psalms, is a fall into imperfection and temporality—into time not yet redeemed, though redeemable by God's mercy. But the fall is less catastrophic in music than in the other arts, because music is comparatively free of the superstition that reality is entirely what it appears to be, finite, bodily, visible, and therefore imitable. If, as Pater says in *Studies in the History of the Renaissance,* all art constantly aspires toward the condition of music, the particular condition so valued is one in which the union of form and matter is most fully achieved. "Art, then, is thus always striving to be independent of the mere intelligence, to become a matter of pure perception, to get rid of its responsibilities to its subject or material." Or, rephrasing Pater, to admit its responsibilities to its subject or material only so far as is consistent with perfection of form.

My father was large: tall but not to excess, not fat or sloppy. He had broad shoulders, as if he were born to appear in uniform. The cloth was a rough serge, set off to advantage by a sergeant's stripes on the left arm. The leather belt was thick; it held a truncheon, itself housed in leather, and a leather pouch of bullets, and on state occasions he wore, again supported by leather, a revolver. He polished belt and boots till they seemed to transcend themselves and become steel. You can't beat leather, as Pinter's Caretaker says. On patrol, my father often brought me along and instructed me to walk in step with him, my shoulders thrust back. My father's uniform had thumb sachets sewn under the armpits, so that when you inserted your thumbs, you had to keep your chest well forward and your shoulders aloft. You had to walk like an officer. My father hated to see anyone stoop-shouldered or with his hands behind his back. I must walk deliberately, my head high, my arms moving in time with the march. I never saw my father strolling or lolling or leaning against a doorpost or with his hands in his pockets. Physically upright, morally upright: he walked the streets as he walked through life, straight ahead, knowing at any moment where he was going and why. He was always on duty, on patrol. I gathered, not from anything he said but from the way he moved, that a firm tread betokened a firm morality. My brother Tim slouched, mainly, I suspect, because he was not on good terms with my father and wanted to goad him. There is a passage in Emerson's *Nature* (1836) about the derivation of moral terms from terms of physical description; "straight" in moral dealing is the spiritual, high-minded correlative of a straight line, the direct tracing of the relation between one point of attention and another. My father was straight in both senses. But straight also means unbending, inflexible, unambiguous. I don't think my father ever contemplated the possibility that there might be merit in not knowing precisely what to make of a situation or in holding loosely in one's mind two rival attitudes. He was afraid of doubt, saw nothing but harm in being of two minds.

Did I exaggerate my father's strength or the moral significance of his bearing? Even now I can't believe I did. So I am shocked to read, in *Moses and Monotheism,* Freud's assertion that "a child's earliest years are dominated by an enormous overvaluation of his father; in accordance with this a king and queen in dreams and fairy tales invariably stand for parents." An overvaluation; in comparison with what? Freud doesn't say what a child's evaluation of his father should be. In the same place he makes another outrageous claim, that "a hero is someone who has had the courage to rebel against his father and has in the end victoriously overcome him."[*] A claim as vulgar as it is insidious.

"I KNOW who is my father's son."[†] It is not clear how this constitutes knowledge or even how it lodges a claim upon knowledge. The words—"my father's son"—stabilise the feelings which occur in their vicinity; the feelings seem to coalesce upon their meaning in that form. If I thought of myself in some other capacity, or in another image, the thought might be more gratifying to me, in one mood or another, but it would not have the force of stability. In another mood I might regard the thought or the image as specious, a flight of bombast. But when I think of myself as my father's son, I feel no inclination to give myself a further characterisation or a greater destiny. Even now, after many years, I have "no better measure of the fitness of things" than the recalled image of my father, in uniform, walking up Charlotte Street toward the square, intent upon his purpose.

SO FAR AS I KNOW, my father's sole illness was the heart attack from which, in a matter of hours, he died. Good health seemed to issue from his nature or his constitution: if he ever had a cold, I have forgotten the occasion. The only theory of health he ever uttered to me was in praise of regular movement of the bowels. He feared constipation. Emerson has a passage in his journal, mocking the barkeepers of the Lafayette Hotel in Salem for coming into the sitting room every five minutes to arrange their hair and collars at the looking glass; and he adds (and later deletes) a remark: "Other men wait upon their bowels most of the day."* My father waited upon them, as if a question of principle were entailed, for the first thirty minutes—if such patience was required— of every day. The lavatory was behind a corner of the bathroom. My father retired to it every morning. He did not lock the door: when I went in, I saw only the day's *Irish Independent,*

Emerson in His Journals, ed. Joel Porte (Cambridge, Mass.: The Belknap Press of Harvard University Press, 1982). Entry for March 5–8, 1836, p. 147.

which he read at stool. He believed that if I warded off constipation and kept up the dose of cod-liver oil, I need not concern myself further with my state of health. He deemed constipation to be the failure of the bowels to move, in a period of twenty-four hours: after that, the matter should be resolved by a single dose of laxative, his favourite being Cascara Sagrada; one spoonful should suffice.

R.U.C. Barracks,
Warrenpoint,
Co. Down
[no date]

Sir:

With reference to the attached application for repayment of Income Tax deducted from my income at the source, I beg to say that my wife and children visited the Irish Free State on a holiday from 3rd. July 1937 to 23rd. August 1937, and resided for part of that time with an uncle, Martin Coady, at Bridge Street, Tullow, Co. Carlow, and with her mother, Mrs. John O'Neill, at 13 Bolton Street, Clonmel, Co. Tipperary. My wife also resided at those places on a holiday for a similar period in each of the years 1936 and 1935, but I do not remember the exact dates. The practice is that during the school holidays in the summer of each year my wife goes to the addresses shown, taking with her the children. The dates vary slightly each year, but generally the duration of their stay is the same. I have no claim to any of these residences, nor does my wife possess any residence or own any property in the Irish Free State. Same the investments shown on this Form. We are resident in Northern Ireland.

Your obedient servant,
Denis Donoghue

KATHLEEN AND MAY were taught piano, but when Gerard Heatley started offering lessons in the violin, I was one of his first pupils. My mother made me a soft cloth pouch which I tied around the chin rest of the violin to protect my sharp collarbone. My fingers, I soon discovered, were too big for the instrument, but I controlled them reasonably well, though not impeccably. I hated practising scales: each note seemed to enter into a competitive relation with its predecessor; there was no joy in the sequence except a formal achievement. I recognised that scales were necessary but otherwise undesirable. Double-stopping proved obdurate: my fingers got in one another's way as I stretched them across the strings. The little finger had virtually no force of pressure, so double-stopping was an unequal struggle, my index and middle fingers making the little finger even frailer than normal. Still, I liked the sounds I made, especially the vibrato. A few years ago, I came across a passage in *The Confessions of Zeno* where Zeno reflects that one's violin resounds so close to the ear that it reaches the heart very quickly. By that comparison, the piano is a distant, unforthcoming instrument, resonances having to pass from the fingertips through several forms of vacancy to a distant destination.

But I soon developed a scruple about vibrato. I began thinking that it was an effeminate habit. I didn't understand why a long note couldn't simply be held, continuous, without flurry. Why did it need to be sent into a swoon? Two or three years ago, I was dismayed to read in Schoenberg's *Style and Idea* an elucidation and a justification of vibrato:

Vibrato consists of a rapid and repeated shift of the point of pressure between finger and string, so it varies, frequently and in quick succession, the length of the string, the pitch of the note; thus its effect is that (instead of their being a single pure tone, as with the open string) a number of others, partly higher, partly lower, surround this pure tone, leaving the ear to seek for itself the middle point of this "simultaneous mass"—to extract the pitch. This makes the tone "living," "interesting," "lively," "warm," and all the rest of it.*

It is not clear to me why the middle point between these extremes is the true tone: the ear, or the mind's ear, must be politically conservative if it seeks the middle point and finds its satisfaction there. Presumably vibrato registers the revulsion the soul feels in the presence of an enforced truth, and yet the ear seeks to arrive at a single truth, by its own adjudication, for each note. The trembling speaks of a more liberal sense of the matter, I suppose. In a kind light, you could regard truth as a middle point discovered between higher and lower approximations.

I have never been convinced. Besides, it must be significant that Schoenberg puts in quotation marks the words "living," "interesting," "lively," and "warm," as if to indicate that these aren't the considerations he would rely upon, but the sort of praise other people commonly give vibrato. I found it significant, too, that vibrato came into its own in the performance of nineteenth-century Romantic music. You could use it even while playing Bach, but it wasn't required. The soul didn't ask for the luxury of hovering between higher and lower tones till Romanticism came to insist upon it as a sign of the freedom and mobility of one's sensibility. If Shelley's "Ode to the West Wind" were music, you would play it with

*Arnold Schoenberg, *Style and Idea* (London: Faber and Faber, 1975), p. 50.

a lot of vibrato. One point I am sure of: if my father had played the violin, he would not have used vibrato.

PLAYING THE VIOLIN was one of the first things I remember doing. It was my first experience of the intrinsic. It did not occur to me to question why I was attempting something in which my skill was meagre. Why try to play the "Méditation" from Massenet's *Thaïs,* since it has been played thousands of times by better violinists? Roland Barthes has remarked that nobody now plays the piano. Youngsters play the guitar—or did, ten or fifteen years ago—but only someone who hopes to be a professional musician learns to play piano or violin. Music is something one listens to, or receives as background felicity, or as a means of passing the time in a car. But the idea of taking up the violin or the piano and going through the tedium of learning to play it has largely gone. Nobody has the patience to practise: scales, arpeggios. The months or years between taking to the violin and reaching the stage of being able to play it badly are among the choice miseries of the young. You lift the instrument, then the bow, bring the bow to the precise degree of tension, apply rosin to it, then tune the strings, repeating the open strings till you have the tuning to perfection. And for what? So that one's playing may be a little less repellent. If your intonation is at fault, at least it is your own fault. You bend over the instrument as if you expected to hear issuing from the sound box the music of the spheres: and what you hear is the same dreariness as yesterday. My fingers were always in the way. The same as yesterday. Yet I did not question the validity of the exercise or the hours spent stumbling over the scales trying to achieve a benign flow of sound.

I suppose the reason why nobody learns to play an instrument is that recordings and tape have made it so easy to listen to perfection. We know that the performances we hear from these sources are at least in part spurious. They are rarely the record of one performance: the sense of their being "live" is a technological feat, not a musical one. But it is easy to forget or ignore this fact. Our relation to these perfections is now a casual one; we take them for granted. It is a relief not to care, not to have to remind oneself that we are listening to a miraculous fraud, a studio technician's magic. The only way of knowing how difficult it is to be perfect in music is by spending time playing badly. A reasonably long time is required. If you take up an instrument and come to the point, within a few days, of producing recognisable, if tedious, sounds from it, you may still believe that with a little more practice you could begin to master it. To dispel this mirage, it is necessary to apply yourself to the instrument for several months or years and to realise how slight the improvement in your playing is; a paler shade of grey.

Barthes's attack on Dietrich Fischer-Dieskau's *lieder*-singing, in comparison with Charles Panzera's, is commonly explained by its disgust: he resented the air of spirituality which Fischer-Dieskau's performances gave, the impression that the sounds came directly from his soul without having to pass through the indignity of a body. Panzera didn't deny the body: you always knew that his sounds issued from throat, larynx, palate, and were propelled and controlled by stomach muscles. F-D's spirituality seemed to claim not only an extraordinary degree of inwardness, but the transcendence of human limitation in every respect. I think there is a simpler explanation for Barthes's attack. As an amateur musician, he resented the impression F-D gives of having mastered the conditions of his art to the point of finding its exercise easy. Panzera always made you feel that it was hard to produce any decent sound and that to do better was a matter of endless labour. Barthes didn't like to think that the supreme achievement of human life is to transcend its conditions: he liked to feel that the world is, upon conviction, worldly; that the human body is indeed a burden to be borne. Panzera made you feel that even the most ethereal sounds are heavy with the weight of every experience they have gone through to become what they are. F-D's sounds, by being or seeming to be effortlessly angelic, can be located only within historical time at a mythic point of childhood or spontaneity. Musically, he seems to have been born without the taint of Original Sin.

I'm not sure that Barthes was right. One rarely hears Panzera, so the comparison is hard to make. One hears nothing but Fischer-Dieskau: his Schubert and Schumann are nearly the only versions one can hear. Not to like his singing is equivalent to not liking James Galway's fluting: it means yielding up virtually every experience of those instruments. But the issue is an ideological one. I wonder, if I had not read Barthes's essay, "The Grain of the Voice," would I have listened differently, as I did at Feldkirch, in August 1988, to Fischer-Dieskau and Peter Schreier? Fischer-Dieskau is tall, handsome, elegant, with an air of high breeding. Recognising the spirituality that Barthes resented, I wondered whether Fischer-Dieskau blithely transcended the worldly labour that went into his skill or arduously refined it out of audible or expressive existence. Peter Schreier is good-looking, too, but squat, in every sense closer to the ground. I did not sense in his performance of *Die Winterreise* any aristocratic hauteur or disdain for the labour and training it entailed. Perhaps these represent two different satisfactions. There may be occasions on which we want to feel that a supreme achievement is simply a gift of God, native to the artist who possesses it; and other occasions, on which we want to feel that native skill has had to be enhanced by work, study, trial, failure, and that it still bears the scar of everything it has gone through.

I am not a good witness. The year in which I laboured over the *Dichterliebe* produced only a patchy account of it. I know how hard it is to sing well, even if one starts with a pretty good voice and endless ambition.

FROM *At Swim-Two-Birds*:

The voice was the first, Furriskey was saying. The human voice. The voice was Number One. Anything that came after was only an imitation of the voice. Follow, Mr Shanahan?

Very nicely put, Mr Furriskey.

Take the fiddle now, said Furriskey.

By hell the fiddle is the man, said Lamont, the fiddle is the man for me. Put it into the hand of a lad like Luke Mac-Fadden and you'll cry like a child when you hear him at it. The voice was number one, I don't deny that, but look at the masterpieces of musical art you have on the fiddle! Did you ever hear the immortal strains of the Crutch Sonata now, the whole four strings playing there together, with plenty of plucking and scales and runs and a lilt that would make you tap the shoe-leather off your foot? Oh, it's the fiddle or nothing. You can have your voice, Mr Furriskey,— and welcome. The fiddle and the bow is all I ask, and the touch of the hand of Luke MacFadden, the travelling tin-smith. The smell of his clothes would knock you down, but he was the best fiddler in Ireland, east or west.

The fiddle is there too, of course, said Furriskey.

The fiddle is an awkward class of a thing to carry, said Shanahan, it's not what you might call a handy shape. They say you get a sort of a crook in the arm, you know. . . .

But the fiddle, continued Furriskey slow and authoritative of articulation, the fiddle comes number two to the voice. Do you mind that, Mr Lamont? Adam sang. . . .

Aye, indeed, said Lamont.

But did he play? By almighty God in Heaven he didn't. If you put your fiddle, Mr Lamont, into the hands of our first parents in the Garden of Eden in the long ago. . . .

They'd hang their hats on it, of course, said Lamont, but still and all it's sweetest of the lot. Given a good player, of course. Could I trouble you, Mr Furriskey?*

THERE WERE NO BOOKS in our house, apart from schoolbooks and the few morally inspiring tracts and novels I got from my uncle. The only book I recall my father owning was *Guide to Careers,* a book that told you how to apply for a job, what the necessary qualifications for the job were, and the address to which to write for an application form. My father had confidence in this work and regularly consulted it to see the jobs for which his children might be qualified. He was not otherwise a reader, having left school when his father died. Thereafter, he took care of the sheep and the mountainy fields and his mother, a tiny woman I met only once, in Killarney; she was dressed entirely in black, boots, skirt, blouse, the whole dominated by a black cloak from head to

*Flann O'Brien, *At Swim-Two-Birds* (London: Longmans Green, 1939), pp. 150–51.

ankle. When my father walked into Killarney to apply to join the RIC, he decided that if he failed he would apply for the Army. He left the land to his brother Peadar. All the remaining brothers and sisters emigrated to America. In one day in 1924 fourteen men left the Black Valley. On the night before they left, they had an American wake, as it was called, so that the emigrants would be too tired and too drunk the following morning to feel their sorrow and fear. My father never travelled farther than Chester, and that only once.

Reading was for my father not difficult but formal. Every morning, immediately after breakfast, in and out of the lavatory, he read *The Irish Independent,* the respectable daily newspaper for Catholics, published in Dublin but distributed through the country. I don't remember hearing him comment upon the news or upon anything he read. The experience of reading it seemed to engross him to the point at which commentary became redundant. When he had occasion to write, he went to his office above the dayroom and settled himself for the task. He rolled up the right sleeve of his shirt and flicked his wrist to prepare for the pen. He had an official writing set, containing an inkwell and a place for pencils and pens. His style was as formal as his bearing in uniform; not copperplate, exactly, but all the letters were joined, the loops precisely turned. I don't know how he acquired his style. Perhaps the ability to write correct English sentences, according to the conventions of the late nineteenth century, was the sole lesson he learned at school. He wrote only in English. He could speak Irish, presumably because he heard enough of it in the Black Valley, but he could neither read nor write it. Not that that was a disability in the North.

THE DAY WE GOT the wireless, I was sent across the square to fetch it. It was too big and heavy to carry, so I was told to wheel the tea trolley and bring the wireless back on it. The square was under repair: or rather, a new surface of tar was being laid upon it and a powder, white or grey, to bind the tar. To protect the men who were working on the job, a wire rope was strung on temporary posts around the section where they were laying the tar. I collected the wireless and started pushing the trolley across the square, and I may have been thinking of something else, but in any case I crashed into the wire rope and fell. The wireless didn't fall off the trolley, but I tore my hands on the wire. Four constituents make the memory of that occasion: the pain of tearing my hand, my crash on the ground, the smell of fresh tar, and the laughter of one of the workers when he saw me falling. His name was Terry O'Neill, the object of the first hatred I remember feeling.

It felt like hatred at the time. Humiliation, I suppose, would sufficiently account for it. I remember reading, a few years ago, perhaps in Peter Ackroyd's biography of T. S. Eliot, that Eliot once, sharing a taxi with Virginia Woolf, was talking about the worst thing. When Mrs. Woolf asked him what he thought was quite the worst, he said: "Humiliation." I suppose the terrible thing about humiliation is the certainty that one is indeed a proper object of ridicule. While it is happening, we can't feel that it will pass, that it's only a wretched moment. It seems to be definitive, the final proof that what one appears to be at that moment is what one is essentially and for all time to come. The reason why Charlie Chaplin's films are loved is that he is often humiliated and yet he picks himself up and trips away, twirling his cane, as if his dignity had merely suffered a temporary setback. It is a necessary element in humiliation, too, that it is always a public event: there must be at least one person to witness it and one to endure it. The private version of humiliation is self-disgust. I'm not sure that there is any relief from that, or a cure. Or how, if the situation is a moral one, remorse comes into it and in the end leaves it. Yeats speaks of forgiving himself, and of dealing imperiously with remorse: "When such as I cast out remorse," he says, and goes on to describe the sweetness that ensues, flowing in his veins. What on earth does he mean? How can anyone cast out remorse? What does it mean for someone to forgive himself? Who am I to forgive myself? I can no more forgive myself than I can forgive Terry O'Neill for laughing at me. It's easier to forgive him because, apart from that incident, I am not implicated in his life or, thank God, he in mine; but I am endlessly implicated in myself.

Some people who are not Catholics think that confession is bound to be an immense release from guilt. Perhaps it is. The priest listens to one's confession, decides that one is genuinely sorry for having offended God, and conveys God's pardon. That's all right for God. But to whom do I confess my humiliations, my self-disgust, my hatred of my body? And who will dispose of the matter by conveying pardon? Whose forgiveness would make any difference?

I MOVED FROM St. Peter's in Warrenpoint to the Christian Brothers' School in Newry, five miles away; perhaps because Mr. Clancy's suicide drew more attention to the school than it could withstand. The school in Newry was called the Carstands, for no reason known to me. Of my months there, I recall nothing except a leathering—four of the best on the right hand by Brother Hennessy—for some misdemeanour. Later we were moved to the new school on the hill above the town, and finally to the Abbey. I went to Newry by bus or bicycle. The bus, coming from Kilkeel and Rostrevor, stopped at the urinal in the centre of the square to pick up passengers. The urinal was mildly sequestered by a ring of trees, and beside it there was a cast-iron watering trough for horses. There were no horses. In the bus the Protestant girls wore brown uniforms and saw no need to talk to the Catholic girls, who wore dark green uniforms. A Protestant girl from Kilkeel, with blond hair cut short and boyish, was reputed to be wild. The Protestant girls sat at the back of the bus and chose not even to notice the Catholic girls and boys who joined the bus at Warrenpoint. When the weather improved, I cycled to and from school, past Narrow Water Castle and Captain Hall's woods.

For about a year I was allowed to go to school by train. The journey took about twelve minutes. No mischief was ever attempted on the way to school, but on the way back it was a common piece of derring-do to open the carriage door when the train started getting up speed, and stretch one's arm to the handle of the next carriage, and show off to the girls by pulling oneself to the point of opening the door of their carriage and descending upon them. There was barely time enough to achieve this feat before the signal box outside the station at Warrenpoint came into sight; but it could be done by a hero. One day the boys in a crowded carriage went mad, and we kicked and smashed the luggage racks.

As a boy, Hopkins asked himself: "What must it be to be someone else?" I have rarely posed the question. It seems trivial to ask: What would it be to be a beautiful, wild girl?

Or even: What would it be to be a beautiful, wild man? It is a more dreadful question to ask: What must it be to be myself and to remember that I was once a boy who helped to smash a railway carriage? What have I done with that violence, unless I still retain it and it takes other forms?

I WORKED HARD at school without thinking of it as work. I was not conscious of being ambitious, or of wanting to do well, or even of imitating my father's zeal in the knowledge that he would be pleased. Whatever the motive was, it had already settled itself in my daily life; a habit, it didn't need to be interrogated or kept up to a mark. I was content to let my life have its definition as work, so that intervals between bouts of study came to appear as lived in the service of work. Jean Dutourd says in *The Man of Sensibility:* "Work brings its own reward, which is a further dose of work."*
There were several subjects at school for which I had little capacity: the mathematical subjects, mostly. But I worked at these, too, and recognised only that my habit had to take a grim turn or enter upon an especially dogged mood before I could take out the textbook in, say, algebra or trigonometry. It didn't occur to me to ask why I should be studying these subjects for which I had no natural talent. One day a boy asked what was the use of studying geometry if you didn't intend being an engineer. The teacher answered: to develop that part of your brain. I found the reason sufficient.

*Jean Dutourd, *The Man of Sensibility,* tr. Robin Chancellor (New York: Simon and Schuster, 1961), p. 153.

I WAS A GOOD READER, or at worst an energetic one. But I see now that my reading was opportunistic: not in the sense of reading one book in preference to another, but in my way of reading. I can't recall a time when I read disinterestedly; I always had a pen and a notebook at hand. If I found something interesting, I'd want to make a note of it. But "interesting" isn't the truth. I went through books looking for whatever I needed. I was never free of purpose. A phrase or a sentence might come in handy for an essay I was writing, some clinching quotation which I could almost fancy, while quoting it, that I had written. If I was not imaginative, I was notionally in the company of those who were: writers, poets especially.

Even now, detective stories are the only fictions I can read without pen and notebook. I am always on the lookout for phrases, as if I lived for the opportunity of using them. "The ministry of carnal perception": it is unlikely that I will have occasion to use that one. On the other hand, Frank Kermode made a distinction, in *The Genesis of Secrecy,* between carnal readings of a text, which are all the same, and spiritual readings, where differences enter. If I could find an occasion for "ministry," I could slip the whole phrase into an otherwise pedestrian sentence. I always suspected, even at school, that this was a pretentious way of reading and that reading was raiding. But nonchalance was hard to acquire.

There are some books that seem to invite an opportunistic reading. One of them, which means a good deal to me in a certain arduous mood, is Emmanuel Levinas's *Totality and Infinity.* I can't read it as a whole, mainly because Jewish-

French intensity oppresses me. I come to certain pages, and my eyes follow the lines, but my mind recedes. Then, without worrying about my failure to cope, I come upon a sentence or a paragraph that lights up the page. I don't believe that the dark passages are dark to every reader or that the bright ones are especially profound. It is more probable that I am reading the book with specific interests which are only occasionally appeased. A theme arises which concerns me, and even the dark is light enough. What I make a note of is not necessarily a passage that clarifies something in my life or some present mundane need, but something that makes it possible for me to think further and to feel that my mind could go a little way on its own. This passage, for instance, on memory:

> By memory I ground myself after the event, retroactively: I assume today what in the absolute past of the origin had no subject to receive it and had therefore the weight of a fatality. By memory I assume and put back in question. Memory realizes impossibility: it assumes, after the event, the passivity of the past, and masters it. Memory as an inversion of historical time is the essence of interiority.*

Not that I really comprehend those sentences or feel that they clear a space to let me through. By whom was the event received if not by a subject? I suppose that Levinas means by a subject a mind with sufficient power of choice to receive or reject an event: in that sense we are rarely subjects when an event impinges upon us. It merely happens, and we are indeed passive in relation to it: therefore the event has the weight of a fatality. I understand that much. Memory, by recalling or recovering an event, removes it from history, at least for the time being. I take it that by "put[ting] back in question"

---

*Emmanuel Levinas, *Totality and Infinity: An Essay on Exteriority,* tr. Alphonso Lingis (Pittsburgh: Duquesne University Press, 1969), p. 56.

Levinas has this act in view. The event, so far as I retrieve it, is now a constituent of my interiority. When I stop thinking about it, it will lapse into historical time again and lose the subjective attention I am giving it. Voluntary memory, I assume. If I recall something involuntarily, a process Proustian in kind if not in quality or degree, fate seems to have given the event a second chance of escaping from historical time. But the quality it has, the quality fate gives it by repetition, is not weight or density: it seems to be involved in a rhythm of remembering and forgetting. If we can't really forget it, it is a case of fixation.

"The weight of a fatality": that weight is something we either want to feel or don't want to feel. If we want to, it is because we need the conviction that our lives are dense, substantial, and all the better for our not having merely invented them. In that mood we like to feel that there are facts or factors which are heavy with their fatality: "They are not to be thought away," as Joyce's Stephen Dedalus says in *Ulysses*. Even at the risk or the cost of their being unassimilable, we want these dense occasions to have occurred. In other moods we want to feel that everything in our lives is, however improbably, our idea, that nothing is opaque to our consciousness. I recognise this latter mood, but I can't praise it: it is vanity, after all, a claim to the angelic mode of knowledge, unmediated.

In *The Use of Poetry and the Use of Criticism* Eliot alludes to an episode, clearly in his own life as a boy on summer vacation in Gloucester, which came into his mind, involuntarily, from time to time:

There might be the experience of a child of ten, a small boy peering through sea-water in a rock-pool, and finding a sea-anemone for the first time: the simple experience (not so simple, for an exceptional child, as it looks) might lie

dormant in his mind for twenty years, and re-appear trans-
formed in some verse-context charged with great imaginative pressure.*

The reappearance first took place in the second part of *Murder
in the Cathedral,* where the Chorus says:

I have lain on the floor of the sea and breathed with the
breathing of the sea-anemone, swallowed with ingurgita-
tion of the sponge. I have lain in the soil and criticised the
worm.

How odd, and oddly inspired, that in a passage in which a
mind imagines participating in the lowest forms of organic
life consistent with their being life at all, Eliot should have
gone from sharing that life—breathed with the breathing of
the sea-anemone—to the highest and most distancing verb of
relatedness—"criticised."

Six years after *Murder in the Cathedral,* in "The Dry Salvages" (1941), the sea-anemone reappeared as one of the
forms—"hints of earlier and other creation"—tossed by the
sea upon the beach:

The starfish, the hermit crab, the whale's backbone;
The pools where it offers to our curiosity
The more delicate algae and the sea-anemone.

—the latter needing no adjective, Eliot's recollection of it
being sufficient.

Eliot was arguing against any attempt to separate imagination from memory; not that he wanted to treat them as one
and the same, but he had his own experience to assure him

*T. S. Eliot, *The Use of Poetry and the Use of Criticism* (London: Faber and Faber,
1964 ed.), pp. 78–79.

that "memory plays a very great part in imagination." The arbitrariness of what we remember and of what we forget seemed to him uncanny:

> Why, for all of us, out of all that we have heard, seen, felt, in a lifetime, do certain images recur, charged with emotion, rather than others? The song of one bird, the leap of one fish, at a particular place and time, the scent of one flower, an old woman on a German mountain path, six ruffians seen through an open window playing cards at night at a small French railway junction where there was a water-mill: such memories may have symbolic value, but of what we cannot tell, for they come to represent the depths of feeling into which we cannot peer. We might just as well ask why, when we try to recall visually some period in the past, we find in our memory just the few meagre arbitrarily chosen set of snapshots that we do find there, the faded poor souvenirs of passionate moments.*

Eliot is content to point to the arbitrary character of these moments; he doesn't pester the subject to explain itself. He doesn't appear to think the principle of the association of ideas is a sufficient explanation. It is interesting that he follows the terminology of depth far enough to refer to "the depths of feeling into which we cannot peer," even though "peering" is what the boy momentously does; because, in other contexts, he trusts rather to the "auditory imagination" to help us when the visual imagination has peered into depths without much satisfaction. In a poet, the auditory imagination involves a feeling for syllable and rhythm, a sense of the primitive and its relation to the highly developed, an ear for the echoes behind words. Eliot remarked the power of Dante's visual sense, but his own imagination wasn't especially visual.

*Eliot, *The Use of Poetry and the Use of Criticism*, p. 148.

He belongs to the tradition in which a writer trusts his ear: Milton, Tennyson, Poe, Swinburne, and Joyce. His essays on Seneca are mainly concerned with the risks—of bravado and self-glorification—a writer in this tradition runs. Seneca's example was often a bad one, especially in Elizabethan and Jacobean tragedy, so it was necessary for Eliot to work out the type of experience the Senecan rhetoric was good for. If Seneca's way with language was entirely sinister, Eliot would have to think again about the development of his own talent, as in "Gerontion."

None of the memories in Eliot's list is in itself remarkable: it is their recurrence that is uncanny. That they had "symbolic value" didn't require him to divine what precisely they symbolised: he was happy enough to feel that they brought a rumour of value. He accepted them and for the same reason trusted to the deliverances of his auditory imagination, which were likely to feel significant if only because they came, if at all, as if from afar and with the force of destiny.

I HATED NEWRY, the Abbey most of all, mainly because it was there I discovered that my body was wrong. When I was twelve, I measured five feet nine, about half an inch shorter than my father. When I was fourteen, I was six feet, Jesus Christ's height, by Christian lore. I stopped at six feet seven. A beanstalk. Hey, mister, is it cold up there? With nothing better to do, Brother Liston summoned me and Matt Durkan to the front of the classroom to be measured. Durkan was usually found to be half an inch taller than I, and even more gangling. His wrists were ambiguously attached to his arms; mine clearly depended from the arms with some show of reason, but his looked as if they could fall off at any moment. The boys cheered the victor. Brother Liston's teeth gleamed as he announced the result, the only occasion on which he disclosed a smile. What must it be to be someone else? What must it be to be Brother Liston?

It is not a matter of being different, in the sense of having a different personality or even a different soul. Mauriac writes somewhere, maybe in *God and Mammon,* that the only tragedy is not to be a saint. The secular version of this tragedy, I suppose, is not to be a genius. I have been content to be neither saint nor genius, though I regularly feel that in doing the discursive things I do, I would give much to do them better. When I read a sentence that I know I could not have written, I feel a blow of envy and direct it, in turn, upon the one who wrote it. When I read Kenneth Burke's *Towards a Better Life,* or Italo Calvino's *Mr. Palomar,* or Italo Svevo's *Confessions of Zeno,* or Primo Levi's *The Periodic Table,* I say to myself: If you only put your mind to it, you could write a book like that. I dally with that fantasy for a few moments till I realise and admit that I could not write one sentence of any of those books. Well, no matter.

Not to be a genius is a bearable affliction. But to be in the wrong body seemed to me, as a boy, to be permanently misshapen. Many years later I settled for the shape and made the wretched best of it. Other things mattered more. But in school, back-to-back against Matt Durkan, nothing mattered more: it was a sufficient humiliation to be there, forced to hold one's head high while Brother Liston put a ruler on me and chalked the line on the yellow wall.

The soul is what refuses the body. What, for instance, refuses to flee when the body trembles, what refuses to strike when the body is provoked, what refuses to drink when the body thirsts, what refuses to take when the body desires, what refuses to give up when the body recoils in horror. These refusals are the prerogative of man. Total refusal is sainthood; looking before leaping is wisdom; and this power of refusal is the soul. The madman has no power of refusal; he no longer has a soul.*

I wonder. It was a disgusting commonplace, ten or fifteen years ago, to claim that madmen—or those supposedly mad or thought to be mad, on socially agreed considerations—had far deeper insight, a greater visionary capacity, than the sane. R. D. Laing and David Cooper lent themselves to this sentiment and did much mischief in the process. Lionel Trilling, slow to anger, denounced Laing and Cooper for their lurid sentimentality. If you have ever looked into the eyes of a mentally ill person, Trilling said, you would have some sense of the appalling loneliness of his condition. Of course the eyes which look, in such cases, are those of a sane man and therefore an incompetent witness. In literature it is customary to

---

*Alain, *Les Arts et les dieux,* ed. Georges Bénézé (Paris: Pléiade ed., 1961), p. 1031: "L'âme c'est ce qui refuse le corps. Par exemple ce qui refuse de fuir quand le corps tremble, ce qui refuse de frapper quand le corps s'irrite, ce qui refuse de boire quand le corps a soif, ce qui refuse de prendre quand le corps désire, ce qui refuse d'abandonner quand le corps a horreur. Ces refus sont des faits de l'homme. Le total refus est la sainteté; l'examen avant de suivre est la sagesse; et cette force de refus c'est l'âme. Le fou n'aucune force de refus; il n'a plus d'âme."

prefer Blake to Wordsworth, Dostoevsky to Tolstoy, finding vicarious satisfaction in experiences we would not choose to have or to suffer.

As a boy, I did not feel that my soul was independent of my body. On the contrary, I felt that it squirmed and shuffled in the monstrous container provided for it. During the war, when clothes were rationed and we had to save up coupons to gain entitlement to them and we had, in any event, little or no money, my mother extended the life of my trousers by adding a swathe of cloth above the waistband. This had the effect of making the fly buttons come in the wrong place and extend beneath my private parts. Taking off and putting on the trousers required opening two ill-adjusted sets of buttons. I wore a long jumper to hide the additional cloth, which was of a different colour and pattern. At school, when I had to use the toilet, I tried to avoid the open receptacles and hovered till a closed stall was free.

I was no good at sports. In the rudimentary gymnasium at the Abbey, I could not climb up the rope or leap onto the parallel bars or do a head-over-heels. Forced to play Gaelic football, I pleaded that because I had to wear glasses, I should not be compelled to play. Brother Newell, who lived for Gaelic football, refused to dispense me from playing. It was a further complication that my brother Tim was not only the best player in the school but probably the best in the whole province, a wizard.

I failed to learn to swim. At the baths in Warrenpoint, Tim pretended to teach me. I wore a loose belt attached to a long pole, which he undertook to hold as I went through the motions of the breaststroke. In the event, he was unreliable, playing the fool; he pretended, convincingly enough, to let me drown by being otherwise engaged, his attention elsewhere, while I was sinking. My body, losing the little faith it had, refused to stay afloat. Shortsighted, I wanted to remain upright in the water and could not work up the courage to put my head even partially under. I wanted to keep at least one foot on the ground. "The Lord upholdeth all that fall and raiseth up all those that He bowed down." Perhaps He did. But what about Tim?

EVEN AS SCHOOLS GO, the Abbey went badly. Brother Cotter taught me English, but not well; mechanically, as if all poems written in the same century were necessarily similar. He gave us several phrases which we could apply, indiscriminately, to poems of the period. "Simplicity, force, and fire in the narrative" was the first attribute of Romantic poetry, and we ended up with "reverence for human nature in itself"; Wordsworth exemplified these and other qualities which I have forgotten. It made no difference whether the poem of the day was "Tintern Abbey" or "Resolution and Independence." Our textbook was an anthology called *The Poet's Company,* which appeared to concentrate, in each case, upon the poet's early writings, as if failure necessarily attended upon development and maturity. "Had I the heavens' embroidered cloths" predominated in the selection from Yeats: no sign of "Among School Children" or "Leda and the Swan" or "Sailing to Byzantium." The only teachers I recall with pleasure and gratitude were Mr. Crinion, who taught us Latin by making Roman literature and society sound interesting and by deducing Latin grammar from Cicero's letters, and Brother Nagle, who was so dissatisfied with the official grammar book of Irish that he composed a new one, somehow stitched the typewritten pages together, and led us through it. We had Mr. Fitzpatrick for Chemistry, my first exemplar of dressing well. He was splendidly groomed, usually wearing a suit—where he got the coupons, I can't say—which shone as if the serge were pleased with its performance, as well it might be. Of his chemistry I can report only that the few experiments we were instructed to perform in the laboratory never produced the right answer, a disability he attributed to variations in the purity of the elements with which we worked. Monsieur Delafaille taught us music, or rather tried without success to persuade a large class of barbarians to listen to the music he played on an organ. One of the indifferent was Gervaise Gibbons, a boy notable not only for the strut of his first name but for the fact that, his father owning a large shop in Newry, he was well dressed and had a watch. On one occasion Monsieur Delafaille used his black strap upon Gervaise Gibbons's hand, missed the crumpled palm, and smashed the watch. Gibbons's father threatened to sue Delafaille and the Christian Brothers for damages, but the case was settled out of court.

At the Christian Brothers', we learned our lessons mainly by memorising them. It was assumed that the first thing to do with a poem was to read it; the next thing, to learn it by heart. On a first reading, you were supposed to work out the meaning of the words and phrases and link the meanings together according to a simple pattern: of beginning, middle, and end if the poem were narrative, or the development of a dominant image if it were a short lyric. But to bring a poem to memory was to take definitive possession of it. While we were learning it by heart, we did not concern ourselves with meaning or with relative emphases, one word taken with another. The meaning of the word was allowed to recede, leaving only the syllables of its name. It was not clear whether we had lost the meaning for good or merely let it float free from the sound of it. We didn't read for the meaning but for the sound, or rather, for the sequence of the sounds. We learned those poems in much the same way in which, in church, we repeated after the priest the Litany of the Blessed Virgin. The phrases were little or nothing in themselves, but our intoning of them, as a congregation, seemed a complete experience. In the litanies the phrases were identical in form; only the words were different in each case. Tower of ivory; house of gold; ark of the covenant; gate of Heaven; morning star—no, that one broke the sequence—help of the afflicted. I had no idea what was meant by ark of the covenant, since we read only the New Testament and were taught to regard the Old as the dark side of life, an occult document which became lucid only when it somehow prefigured the life and work of Christ. For all I knew of the ark of the covenant, ark might just as well have been arc, a curve or trajectory. The words of a poem in English, Irish, or Latin could be intoned in the same spirit: the meaning could be left to take care of itself; what we didn't know of it wouldn't hurt us. Like a proper name, each word was complete in itself; its acoustic character had some relation to the feeling it denoted, but not one we had to ponder.

I did not question the value of committing poems to memory or of letting the meanings of the words slide into parentheses while the memorisation was going on. I think I knew that by learning the words as names, I could recover the meaning at any point and with little trouble.

In the same spirit, learning a Shakespeare play entailed memorising its main speeches, nearly everything except the stage directions, and staying within the words. There was no classroom discussion. When we recited Shylock's speech—

I am a Jew. Hath not a Jew eyes? Hath not a Jew hands, organs, dimensions, senses, affections, passions; fed with the same food, hurt with the same weapons, subject to the same diseases, heal'd by the same means, warm'd and cool'd by the same winter and summer, as a Christian is? If you prick us, do we not bleed? If you tickle us, do we not laugh? If you poison us, do we not die? And if you wrong us, shall we not revenge? If we are like you in the rest, we will resemble you in that. . . .

—we did not pursue the matter into considerations of Jews and Christians, the status of the Jew in Elizabethan or Venetian society, the nature of justice and of mercy. The meaning of a passage was allowed to reside in the words as the juice resides in an orange: eat the orange and you get the juice. I am not sure that Brother Cotter, whom otherwise I remember harshly, was wrong: at least we were in no danger of turning a play into an editorial, engaging in arguments about equity and revenge which could have proceeded just as fruitfully without reference to the play.

What remains from my experience of reading literature at school I can hardly say. I can't regard it as a loss that there was no argument or even that poems sank into my mind as words and phrases largely independent of their contexts, nearly as free as music: else a great prince in prison lies; through the dear might of him that walked the waves; this ecstasy doth unperplex; we receive but what we give; though worlds of wanwood leafmeal lie; woods decaying, never to be decayed; shall I abide in this dull world which in thy absence is no better than a sigh?

One of the poems in *The Poet's Company* which we were required to learn by heart was Keats's "Ode on a Grecian Urn."

Brother Cotter: "'Heard melodies are sweet, but those unheard are sweeter.' What does 'those unheard' mean?"

Gerry Small: "Songs he didn't hear."
Brother Cotter: "And why were they sweeter?"
Gerry Small: "I don't know, sir."

Not that it is entirely clear. It is true that the first stanza talks of two different degrees of sweetness:

Sylvan historian, who canst thus express
A flowery tale more sweetly than our rhyme:

This may mean only that Greek statuary maintained the decencies of pastoral sentiment better than modern English poetry manages to do. But in any case it introduces the motif of two levels of expression and immediately attributes them to "men or gods." The erotic decipherings—"What maidens loth? . . . What wild ecstasy?"—show the sort of thing that men and women run to, and don't degrade them for it, but the hectic rush of the lines makes it reasonable to keep the two levels in view while backing off from one of them. After the sexual interpreting, the second stanza distances itself from the rout:

Heard melodies are sweet, but those unheard
Are sweeter; therefore, ye soft pipes, play on;
Not to the sensual ear, but, more endear'd,
Pipe to the spirit ditties of no tone:

It is cooler play, enforced by the internal rhyme of "heard" and "unheard," the visual pun of "unheard" and "ear," and the sounding pun of "ear" and "endear'd," the last of these making the comparative ("more endear'd") say that the ditties of no tone are more precious than the audible kind because they have a better class of audience ("the spirit," not "the sensual ear"). The stanza is poised on a present moment, tense between the alternatives ("men or gods") that the urn and the mind looking at it seem to offer. Keats is writing a poem to say that, taking one consideration with another, the silence of Greek statuary has an advantage over the flushed garrulousness of poetry.

Kenneth Burke, thinking of the two levels and the melodies heard and unheard, says that "the poet whose sounds are the richest in our language is meditating upon absolute sound, the essence of sound, which would be soundless as the prime mover is motionless, or as the 'principle' of sweetness would not be sweet, having transcended sweetness."* But the trouble with this reading is that if you completely separate the sensual ear from the spirit, you make the poem sound priggish. It is justified by the men-or-gods, which doesn't allow for a third state, but it makes the men seem like boys bent over a radio and the gods seem intolerably rarefied.

The problem begins with "those unheard." Unheard has a rather small range of meanings, Shakespeare's three covering most of the field. It can mean (1) not heard because defeated by something far louder, as in the storm of *Pericles*:

> *The seaman's whistle*
> *Is as a whisper in the ears of death,*
> *Unheard.*

Or (2) not attended to when it should have been, like the bad news King John refused to hear till the Bastard rebuked him:

> *But if you be afeard to hear the worst,*
> *Then let the worst unheard fall on your head.*

*Kenneth Burke, *A Grammar of Motives* (New York: George Braziller, 1955), p. 449.

Or (3), a variant of (2), where the refusal to hear unwelcome news amounts to a refusal to admit to one's presence the one who brings it. When Caesar sends word to Cleopatra that "she shall not sue unheard" if she gets rid of Antony in Egypt, he means that even then she'll have to beg his pardon, and while he won't send her away unheard, it will be a signal act of magnanimity on his part that he receives her.

None of these meanings fits the phrase in Keats: it doesn't mean melodies played so *pianissimo* that they are inaudible or melodies that should be listened to but aren't. "Those unheard" may indeed be absolute sound and therefore soundless, as Burke thinks, but the only way to make the passage spiritually unpretentious, while keeping it high-minded, is by taking the "spirit" to mean the poetic imagination or inspiration as distinct from the ordinary sensory capacities. The lines seem to be saying that there must be feelings superior to those occasioned by ordinary seeing and hearing, even though we may not have reliable access to them. They have to be there if the notion of imagination is to be taken seriously as well as coolly. The pipe-playing figures on the urn give Keats warrant for saying that just as the mind's eye works when we close our eyes, so the mind's ear when we imagine the sounds it might attend to. At the end of the stanza he begins to assess more ruefully the price that has to be paid for any felicity.

But the *un-* prefix in English is difficult, apart from the difficulty we find in Keats's version of it. The most natural form of the prefix is one in which something is done and then, as upon a second thought, retracted. This is exactly rendered in the verb "to undo"; you do something, then you take it back or dismantle it; you are perplexed till this ecstasy unperplexes. It is a piquancy that the second thought is enacted in the first syllable, and the effect is one of cancellation. But in other cases the problem is to know what status the verb continues to have even after you've retracted or otherwise erased it. When E. E. Cummings used such a homemade word as "unman"—a noun, in his usage, not a verb—he meant someone who should have been manly but wasn't. But sometimes the notion given in the verb stays in the air of the meaning longer than it should and is not really removed by the prefix. In *The Waste Land* "the young man carbuncular" seducing the typist makes certain gestures which "still are unreproved, if undesired." "Unreproved" suggests that she should have reproved them but couldn't be bothered, so let him go ahead. The notional "reproved" is held pending, even after it has supposedly been erased by the *un-*; the ethical issue has not been removed. But "if undesired" isn't as straight-forward. The parallel character of the phrasing, the rhyme between unreproved and undesired, gives both root-verbs the same status. But in the poem they can't have the same status. She should have reproved his gestures; she should never have desired them. The prosaic sense is: by putting a stop to his probings, she should have shown him that, apart from other considerations, she didn't want them. That suggests the mean-ing: "which still are unreproved even if they are not desired." But "not desired" isn't the same as "undesired"; the first discounts any suggestion of her ever having wanted the man's attentions; the second implies that they were or might have been desired, but that she had second feelings about them, largely of indifference. The point is that English doesn't easily distinguish between "not known" and "unknown," "not heard" and "unheard."

Eliot is to the point because so much feeling in his poems is indeterminate, wandering between two possible forms, either of which would be misleading. The reason why he fusses, in his dissertation on Bradley's philosophy, between the demands of subject and of object is that each of these offers itself far more insistently than he can allow. He has to say to each of them, "You are not precisely what I feel at all, not at all." His typical device, in the poems, is to hold a word only long enough to start withdrawing it or undermining its certitude. In "Burnt Norton" the "unheard music hidden in the shrubbery" is anticipated by the experiences which were thought of but in the end set aside; the passage which we did not take, the door we never opened. The music has virtual status, in a sense beyond Langer's; it might have been heard but wasn't, a condition emphasised by transposing it from a sound to an object, "hidden in the shrubbery." The relation between the prefix and the root-verb is a subjunctive one, along a narrative line: we might have heard the music, but didn't, either because its sounds were too rarefied, like the music of the spheres, or we weren't quite ready for them. In "East Coker" "undeceived" is simple:

> *We are only undeceived*
> *Of that which, deceiving, could no longer harm.*

The knowledge we derive from experience is useless because as soon as we start relying upon it, the situation to which we apply it has changed. We can only detect ourselves, remove ourselves from the particular enchantment, when the situation has changed so much that the notion we had of it no longer matters. The meaning has escaped. In "The Dry Salvages"

> *. . . the torment of others remains an experience*
> *Unqualified, unworn by subsequent attrition*

precisely because it is not one's own; if it were one's own, it would already have begun to be qualified, worn, "covered by the currents of action." Later in "The Dry Salvages," "the unattended moment" is like the seducer's unreproved gestures; we should attend to it but don't. The same in "Little

Gidding": the "spirit unappeased" should be appeased but isn't; the condition is "unflowering" because it should have flowered but hasn't: it should flower as in memory:

> For liberation—not less of love but expanding
> Of love beyond desire, and so liberation
> From the future as well as the past.

There is no rule for these undoings. Eliot's early poetry is uncanny, uncannily haunting, because it inhabits the English language as a ghost might walk through a graveyard; it seems to need expressive resources which the language has set its face against. It is a poetry of arrested gestures, declined certitudes, phrasings so discontented with themselves that they stay only long enough to have been there. When we call his later poems, on the whole, discursive, we mean that they settle, however ruefully, for the little the English language is willing to give—the choice between "do" and "undo" is a blunt one—and appease themselves by reflecting that in the end the poetry does not matter.

FROM ELIOT'S ESSAY on Thomas Heywood, author of *A Woman Killed with Kindness:*

Heywood's is a drama of common life, not, in the highest sense, tragedy at all; there is no supernatural music from behind the wings. He would in any age have been a successful playwright; he is eminent in the pathetic, rather than the tragic. His nearest approach to those deeper emotions which shake the veil of Time is in that fine speech of Frankford which surely no men or women past their youth can read without a twinge of personal feeling:

> *O God! O God! that it were possible*
> *To undo things done; to call back yesterday. . . .**

IT SEEMED NATURAL, having committed poems to memory, to recite them aloud, and I enjoyed doing this: it was like playing the violin, except that I had some flair for it. It seemed a fine thing to keep the metres going while attending to the sense of the sentence. I am not sure that the poems I liked best to recite were in every case the poems I liked best to know and to remember. For recitation, a certain grandiloquence is permitted, and it is most agreeable if the high notes are clearly in the poem rather than in the ardour of the speaker:

> *Call us what you will, we'are made such by love;*
> *Call her one, me another fly,*
> *We'are Tapers too, and at our own cost die.*

Donne doesn't invite a demure or subdued reading. Eliot said that the really fine rhetoric in Shakespeare's plays occurs when a character sees himself in a dramatic light, as Donne's speaker does. It seems appropriate that the consumed lovers should die with their illumination and that the metrical line should end upon that death. The fact that the line is, except for "Tapers," entirely a sequence of monosyllables makes it relentless.

The other cadence I recall liking was one in which the music

---

*T. S. Eliot, *Selected Essays* (London: Faber and Faber, 1951), p. 181.

is varied within a pattern which it doesn't disrupt, as in Book Three of *Paradise Lost:*

> *. . . and in his face*
> *Divine compassion visibly appeared,*
> *Love without end, and without measure Grace.*

The last line is enclosed by monosyllables equally grand, but within that embrace the music is full of grace notes—the division of the line into two parts, four syllables followed by six; the doubt, which doesn't amount to an equivocation, about the chief meaning of end—is it termination or purpose? The moral absolutes change places, "Love" coming at the beginning of its phrase, "Grace" at the end of its differently weighted phrase. Grace is indeed given to us without measure, since if it were measured according to our deserts, we might not get any.

AT SCHOOL IN NEWRY, I sensed that in some respects I differed from my colleagues, but I did not feel that the difference amounted to much in my favour. I knew that my intelligence was not of a creative kind. I did not even try to write a poem or a story. My mind was usually engaged in considering the work or bearing of someone else; my father in the first instance, certain writers thereafter. My stance was retrospective. If I formulated an idea, it seemed merely to name feelings that hardly went in need of naming. The best fortune they aspired to was adequacy: they were good enough if they were justly responsive to something someone else had done. They did not compel into existence any feelings otherwise silent or repressed. Many years later, I recognised this limitation so frequently that I believed it decisive; it is a limitation in discursiveness itself, that it comments on everything and has nothing better to do. There is a passage in Paul Klee's diary where he talks about the empty spaces left to chance:

> It is necessary never to work toward a conception of the picture completely thought out in advance. Instead, one must give oneself completely to the developing portion of the area to be painted. The total impression is then rooted in the principle of economy; to derive the effect of the whole from a few steps.*

A few steps, a hunch, a swift stroke, not the whole canvas filled with forethought. It is the distinction between *concetto* and *immagine: concetto* is a free act of creation, full of confidence in possibilities at any moment undefined, a notion, an idea for a poem, trusting to the future; *immagine* is the idea which identifies something already complete except for the formulation; it merely annotates something that sustains the annotation without needing it. I would like to have lived with *sprezzatura,* cutting a dash: my talents are such as to express themselves in circumspection.

It did not grieve me that I lacked inventiveness, could not make up a story or imagine a sequence of thoughts requiring rhyme. All I wanted was to observe a relation be-

---

*The Diaries of Paul Klee: 1898–1918, ed. Felix Klee (Berkeley: University of California Press, 1964), pp. 235–36.

tween myself and structures I had not invented. Tolstoy says somewhere that his freedom consisted "in my not having made the laws."* Presumably he was free to obey them or, at his risk, to reject them. When I think of my early years, I find myself always in relation to something I revered precisely because its existence and force were independent of my will. I played music, observed the score, attentive to the composer's will as the form of the music embodied it. I liked poems more than novels or short stories because their formal character was more completely in evidence. I admired the dogmas and doctrines of the Church all the more because they did not consult my interests. I revered the law because my father administered it and bore witness to its integrity. Mine was the intelligence that comes after.

TWO SENTENCES FROM *Totality and Infinity* stay in my mind. The first: "The inner life is the unique *way* for the real to exist as a plurality." In Western philosophy the real has been deemed to exist, if at all, as a singularity, because the paradigm of existence is the existence of something, either an object or something analogous to an object. The privileging of the sense of sight is based upon that prejudice; seeing is authenticating. If I see an object, the object exists and so do I. The test case of an active human presence in the world is that of a subject apprehending an object. Emerson is unusual

*Quoted in John Bayley, *The Order of Battle at Trafalgar, and Other Essays* (London: Collins Harvill, 1987), p. 216.

in distinguishing between the horizon and the particular farms which constitute it. The farms belong to several people, but the horizon is free to anyone's possession. Normally, the experience of a single subject in relation to a single object is thought to be the basic figure of human presence. One result is that the real is supposed to offer itself to perception as a singularity; this object, this thing, this person we look at. The real does not exist as a plurality when we look at one thing, and then another, and so forth: each of these is singular, and is never anything else. It is weird that there is something rather than nothing. No wonder the experience of apprehending the things that exist is so privileged. But only the inner life, as Levinas says, is constituted as a plurality: we register that condition by saying that the contents of the inner life are not objects but relations, and that they may just as easily be wilful, arbitrary, and promiscuous as single-minded. If the official aim were not knowledge, the paradigm of a mind taking possession of an object would lose its privilege. But it is hard for us to imagine any purpose other than that of knowledge: hence the regularity with which such philosophers as Levinas, Marcel, and Buber represent the act of knowing as if it were not—or not merely—epistemological. In *I and Thou* the object of knowledge, so far as it is "you" or "thou," is the partner of my acknowledgement: it is not a matter of apprehension, knowledge, seizure. So to Levinas's second sentence: "The essence of discourse is ethical." As a consequence, Levinas doesn't speak of knowledge and its object or of meaning on the analogy of cognitive seizure: meaning, for him, is the face of someone else, coming into one's view. He refers to "the primordial face-to-face of language,"* primordial because nothing more fundamental can be imagined.

*Levinas, *Totality and Infinity,* pp. 58, 216, 206.

I SUPPOSE I DREAMED, but on awaking, nothing remained but a vague sense of having dreamed. Except for one recurrent nightmare, I retained only a vague sense of turbulence, of a night spent busily but fruitlessly. The exception was, any reader of Freud would say, banal. I climbed a tower. Ireland has two kinds of towers: the Norman tower, exemplified by Yeats's tower at Ballylee, squat, low, built for defence against an enemy already at hand; and the Celtic, or round, tower, high and thin, the stones rounded, built for defence against an enemy still far off. My dream tower was the Celtic round tower. The steps led me to the top: it was impossible to resist them. From the top, with such inevitability that an accomplished dreamer would have foreseen the event, I fell to the ground. When I woke up, Tim was, as usual, in the valley of the bed. I looked out the window, seeing only the shadow of the telephone exchange at the bottom of the garden. Even then I was shortsighted.

I HAVE BEEN THROUGH *Totality and Infinity* again. Some of the passages I have marked, in earlier reading, now seem just as opaque as those I have passed over in bewildered silence. Other passages strike me as lucid and suggestive. As a gloss, for instance, on the sentence about the inner life and existence as plurality, the following passage is worth transcribing:

Interiority is the very possibility of a birth and a death that do not derive their meaning from history. Interiority constitutes an order different from historical time, in which totality is constituted, an order where everything is *pending,* where what is no longer possible historically remains always possible.*

By "history" I presume he means: that which produces the future. Something comes into history by playing a part in the production of the future. If it doesn't do that, it merely enhances the moment in which it is entertained. But Levinas is tender toward such experiences. The historian has no time for them, since they didn't come into historical time. Levinas recovers the dignity of the inner life, so that such experiences may regain their self-respect. History is only one way of being significant. Memory gives the unofficial sense of history, effects an order not sequential but agglutinative. That is why we never ask our memories to line up rationally or sequentially, like soldiers on parade: they obey our orders, but not always or in the form we prescribe.

I MADE LISTS OF WORDS, with the intention some day of using them in sentences. Most of them were of Latin origin: curial, solicitude, sophistry, profane, vibration, tenacity, vivacity—ideally, in the sense in which Arnold somewhere speaks of striking interventions or phrasings as vivacities—regnant, rebarbative, exorbitant. I have managed to find sentences for nearly all of these, often at some cost to the order

*Ibid., p. 56.

of the argument. Some words on the list are too rarefied to be feasible: benison, tenebrous, squamous, armature. Wallace Stevens wrote that "the squirming facts exceed the squamous mind," and I am sure they do, "squamous" meaning stratified, laminated, or otherwise layered. It is piquant that squirming is the lower-class or repellent version of sinuous, and sinuous is what squamous things like snakes are praised for being. I suppose I could use "armature" to describe some situation in a poem, but Hugh Kenner has used it in that connection so regularly that it belongs to him.

Some words I can't use because, when I was a boy, they meant alien things. If you are a member of a choir, you are a chorister, but in Warrenpoint and, I suppose, in other places, too, a chorister was a member of a choir in a Protestant church. The Catholic version was choirboy. When I came to Dublin and started studying music with Brian Boydell, one of my colleagues was a man named Frank Keyte, clearly a Protestant, as his manner and bearing indicated; but when I inquired what he did for a living, he said: "I'm a chorister in St. Patrick's." Once when I was talking in a class at University College, Dublin, about Shakespeare's sonnet "That time of year thou mayst in me behold," I found myself on the edge of saying that the "sweet birds" referred to in the poem are the choristers in the choir stalls and stopped myself just in time. I couldn't bring myself to say the word "chorister," and justified myself to myself by thinking that the "bare ruin'd choirs where late the sweet birds sang" refers to Catholic monasteries or churches before the destruction of the monasteries and the regnant barbarism of the King.

I TRANSCRIBED FINE SENTENCES and stanzas so that I might the more thoroughly remember them, but also for the satisfaction of embodying a privileged relation to their merit. I had not composed any of those splendid pieces, but at least I could claim the distinction of having appreciated them. They were, in that limited but not disgraceful sense, my property. I had a better claim to them than anyone else had, apart from the author in each case. I could even fancy that everyone in the world had read them and failed to see their magnificence. So I laboured over the transcriptions as if I were a scribe bent over his vellum, tracing the characters and adorning them. Besides, penmanship was a skill in high repute during those years, presumably for the last time. I don't find it absurd that Bouvard and Pécuchet, having presumed to make a new life for themselves and to appropriate the enormously increased range of knowledge in their time, should find the experience futile in the end and return to the mundane occupation—scrivening—from which they had hoped to escape. *Copier comme autrefois:* all they need now is a two-seater desk. With the customary utensils—*achat de registres et d'ustensiles, sandaraque, grattoirs, etc.*—they set to work—*Ils s'y mettent.*

EMPSON HAS A PASSAGE IN *Some Versions of Pastoral* about childhood: he is thinking of the sentiments and notions that got into the *Alice* books as if from a gap between Wordsworth and Darwin. He refers to a feeling, pervasive in Wordsworth and Coleridge but found earlier, too, "that no way of building up character, no intellectual system, can bring out all that is inherent in the human spirit, and therefore that there is more in the child than any man has been able to keep." The idea of the child, "that it is in the right relation to Nature, not dividing what should be unified, that its intuitive judgment contains what poetry and philosophy must spend their time labouring to recover, was accepted by Dodgson and a main part of his feeling."* Empson makes a point of this because he is convinced that any life is bound to exhibit waste: only a small fraction of anyone's possibilities can ever be realised. Yeats tried to take the harm out of this fatality by developing a rhetoric of excess, making "wasteful" a sign of endless energy available. "Only the wasteful virtues earn the sun." The opposite of that "wasteful" is not niggardly or penurious but frugal, economical, making the expenditure of spirit tally with the object on which it is spent. Like Blake in this, Yeats was never satisfied with anything less than nimiety: it wasn't good enough till it became too much of a good thing in someone else's eyes.

The reason why, even in secular terms, we are encouraged now and again to think about death is that we prompt ourselves to know that we're not eternal and that further waste of our possibilities should be stopped. A secularist has to ask of anyone's life: To what extent did it fulfil its potentiality? The criteria for such a consideration are likely to be formal or otherwise aesthetic: Had the life a coherent shape, a form, or did it merely break off? A Christian's conviction impels him to ask, chiefly of his own life: Has it been a valid preparation for the true life to come, when the soul may hope to enjoy

*William Empson, *Some Versions of Pastoral* (London: Chatto and Windus, 1950), pp. 260–61.

the eternal presence of God? The shape is not considered, since the life is to be completed only "in our next."

I find it hard to worry about the waste of my life in any sense: it didn't start with many possibilities. For my father and mother it began with my birth: every day they had to take care of me, foster me. It began, for me, with the first moment I remember, my brother's death when I was four years old. The site of my possibility coincided with the end of his; except that we believe, as Catholics, that he is in Heaven. I began to live from that moment, earlier moments being merely notional. But my beginning was already a direction; I was moving toward certain fulfilments or frustrations. The goal was implicit in my beginning, its nature and scope largely determined by the conditions of my growing up in Warrenpoint to parents Denis and Johanna Donoghue, subject to the constraints which I have only to name my parents in this way to recall.

I SOMETIMES WONDER what I have missed by not reading fairy stories as a child. What would it have meant to have my early life suffused with stories, magical occurrences and transformations? A few years ago, I read the stories of George Macdonald because I was invited to write something about them in the *New York Review of Books:* to come to them for the first time, as an adult, made me try to imagine what it would have been like to read them as a child. I have never been able to tell a story or even to recall one. Jokes fall out of my mind almost as soon as I have heard them. Plots of the novels I have read, studied, and written about are the first parts I forget. Chapters stay in my mind, fragments of conversation, a descriptive passage here and there, but I would be hard put to recite the plot of even the standard masterpieces. Don't ask me to recall the plot of *Pride and Prejudice*. Do parents still tell their children bedtime stories? I doubt it. I never told any of my children a story or read to them a chapter of a novel. To think of all the things I haven't done. I wonder have I lived a life without air, not enough oxygen or light or ease or fantasy. Auden distinguished between the primary world in which people have to live with their bodily needs and habits, and the secondary world in which they live, if they can, upon dreams or magic or illusion or supposition. The difference between my life and my father's life is, I think, considerable. His life had no secondary component, so far as I could see: primary needs engrossed him from morning to night. By my own effort and by the facilities he made available to me, in education chiefly, I have been able to live to some extent in both a primary and a secondary world. But I seem to have constrained my sense of the secondary world by criteria founded upon the primary one and its needs. Isn't it silly that opera means nothing to me; that oratorios seem alien to me because most of them are Protestant; that I have only once, and recently, seen *The Wizard of Oz*? What am I preserving my *gravitas* for?

I HAVE DOUBTED the veracity of Wordsworth's *The Prelude* in one episode, where he describes how, as a boy, he saw a drowned man's body dragged up from a lake. He was not terrified, he reports; the reading of fairy stories had filled his mind with such images. There are various possibilities. Wordsworth, reading those fairy stories as a boy, converted them into images with such imaginative force that no real events could exceed the fictive ones. When he saw a drowned man's body, he merely verified or repeated what he had imagined, as if he had conjured into existence the drowned corpse. Another possibility is that nothing he encountered in reality was as vivid to him as what he imagined, that an image he had merely to transcribe never rivalled the images he had conjured. The image of the drowned man necessarily coincided with itself; it was merely what it was: unlike the imagined figments, which were anything and everything they might in any context be.

And yet: what is the quality of the imagination that fails—or refuses—to distinguish between an imagined corpse and a real one? If it fails, no moral question arises. But if it refuses, the refusal means that it prefers its own figures or figments to any that may be delivered to it contingently. In Yeats's terms, the antithetical mind prefers its own images to any primary images, since primary images are merely received; antithetical images are one's own peremptory creations. From Nietzsche and Yeats to Harold Bloom, there is a strong tradition—or at least a tradition that proclaims its strength—according to which the supreme power is one's own vital spark, which Emerson called one's *pneuma.* Bloom takes pride as well as pleasure in distinguishing *pneuma,* or spark, from *psyche,* or soul; mainly, I think, because the *pneuma* evades moral judgment while the *psyche* is exposed to that judgment. The same tradition exalts genius above all moral consideration and, especially in Bloom, takes Milton's Satan as its supreme type, the "egotistical sublime" which can't be called into question, even by God.

Still, the passage in *The Prelude* is bizarre:

> *The succeeding day,*
> *(Those unclaimed garments telling a plain Tale)*

Went there a Company, and, in their Boat
Sounded with grappling irons, and long poles.
At length, the dead Man, 'mid that beauteous scene
Of trees, and hills and water, bolt upright
Rose with his ghastly face; a spectre shape
Of terror even! and yet no vulgar fear,
Young as I was, a Child not nine years old,
Possess'd me; for my inner eye had seen
Such sights before, among the shining streams
Of Fairy Land, the Forests of Romance:
Thence came a spirit hallowing what I saw
With decoration and ideal grace;
A dignity, a smoothness, like the works
Of Grecian Art, and purest Poesy. *

It starts going wrong with "telling a plain Tale," since the phrase refers to the truth of the event and, at the same time, assimilates that truth to a narrative not at all plain. The juxtaposition of the beautiful—"that beauteous scene"—and the sublime—"Rose with his ghastly face"—is also too engagingly poetic. The damage is completed with "vulgar": "and yet no vulgar fear" can't mean anything better than "and yet no commonplace fear such as those would feel who haven't read fairy tales and don't know the difference between the beautiful and the sublime." This whole book of *The Prelude* is called "Books," and the point of it is to show the rich, imaginative continuity between the images which arise from daily events and those produced by books. But there is something distasteful in Wordsworth's way of distinguishing his sensation from vulgar fear: distasteful, too, in his explaining the self-possession by distinguishing the eye from "my inner

*William Wordsworth, *The Prelude* (text of 1805), ed. Ernest de Selincourt, new corrected ed. by Stephen Gill (London: Oxford University Press, 1970), Book V, lines 466–81, p. 80.

eye." Besides, what his inner eye saw—"such sights"—was not the same as the drowned man's ghastly face: there is nothing "such" about a particular man's face, except in the abstracting mind of someone past caring to retain the true distinction. The claim made in "hallowing" is disgraceful, because only a false spirituality would take pleasure in disposing of the event by aestheticising it, sending it on its urbane way to "Grecian Art, and purest Poesy." In other parts of *The Prelude* Wordsworth knows he is being smug and detects himself, but not here.

THE *Philosophical Investigations* of Wittgenstein begins with a quotation from Augustine's *Confessions:*

I can remember that time, and later on I realized how I had learnt to speak. It was not my elders who showed me the words by some set system of instruction, in the way that they taught me to read not long afterwards; but, instead, I taught myself by using the intelligence which you, my God, gave to me. For when I tried to express my meaning by crying out and making various sounds and movements, so that my wishes should be obeyed, I found that I could not convey all that I meant or make myself understood by everyone whom I wished to understand me. So my memory prompted me. I noticed that people would name some object and then turn towards whatever it was that they had named. I watched them and understood that the sound they made when they wanted to indicate that particular thing was the name which they gave to it, and their actions clearly showed what they meant, for there is a kind of universal language, consisting of expressions of the face and eyes, gestures and tones of voice, which can show whether a person means to ask for something and get it, or refuse it and have nothing to do with it. So, by hearing words arranged in various phrases and constantly repeated, I gradually pieced together what they stood for, and when my tongue had mastered the pronunciation, I began to express my wishes by means of them. In this way I made my wants known to my family and they made theirs known to me, and I took a further step into the stormy life of human society, although I was still subject to the authority of my parents and the will of my elders.*

It is a problem, but not a disability, that Augustine's account of learning his native language depends upon an unexplained theory of memory—the explanation comes later—and upon an equally unexplained account of "language as gesture." How did he know that those particular gestures—turning toward an object, and so on—drew attention to those objects and not to other things that might be in their vicinity? It is all to the good that the acquisition of a language is based upon a metabiology rather than a metaphysics, an ontology, or an epistemology. The notion of a universal language is more plausible if it is based upon the assumption—elaborated by Kenneth Burke—that we are bodies that learn language, than upon a theory of linguistic spirituality. We are bodies, and inasmuch as we are human bodies, we have the capacity to learn to speak. What we learn is always already there; we come into our native language.

Wittgenstein comments on the passage from the *Confessions*:

Augustine describes the learning of human language as if the child came into a strange country and did not understand

*Augustine, *Confessions,* tr. R. S. Pine-Coffin (Harmondsworth, Eng.: Penguin Books, 1961), Book I, ch. 8, p. 29.

the language of the country; that is, as if it already had a language, only not this one. Or again, as if the child could already *think,* only not yet speak. And "think" would here mean something like "talk to itself."*

Presumably Wittgenstein's "had a language" is the same as Augustine's "universal language," language as bodily gesture, semantic mimicry. It is a comfort to us to discover that our gestures are the same: differences between one language and another arise later.

Wittgenstein's idea of thinking as something like talking to oneself is charming, but it doesn't say whether a child talks to himself according to a "language as gesture" or according to an *ur*-vernacular prefiguring the one he eventually comes into. I would like to think that our being bodies gives us the grammar of a universal language and that anything more formal is only a development of this, but I don't know what would constitute evidence. Can thinking go on without a vernacular, however rudimentary? If an infant falls and cries, has he or she already come into a metabiological language of cries that entail thinking? Are the limits of a language the limits of a world only when someone decides to mark those limits or to stake a claim to them?

I don't know the answers to any of these questions. But I can't see why people who insist on the linguistic constraints of thinking seem to think of this as a frightful privation, and take grim pleasure in it.

Presumably the point of learning another language is that it helps you to surmount the prejudices of your own; like coming into a foreign country and seeing that, yes, it's different but in some ways contiguous to your own, as if you already had a language "but not this one." The problem with

*Ludwig Wittgenstein, *Philosophical Investigations,* tr. G. E. M. Anscombe (Oxford: Basil Blackwell, 1968), pp. 15–16.

speaking English as a native in Warrenpoint was that I knew it wasn't—or wasn't entirely—my language. I spoke it not with a bad accent but with bad faith.

LATIN WAS MY FAVOURITE SUBJECT. I took pleasure in its air of stability, its unfussy precision, its sense of holding its constituents in well-judged relations. Besides, I liked to feel that meanings were waiting in a great language to be discovered and that the phonetic character of the words held open the possibility of further developments. I did not like to assume that it was necessary to decide, in advance, what you wanted to say and then try to say it through the instrumentality of the language at hand. Much better to trust to the luck of the draw and find among the words themselves the meanings that could be produced from their internal resources. The Latin teacher, Mr. Crinion, drew attention to a passage from Saint Augustine's *Confessions* where the meaning issues from the possibility of using a word first literally and then, in the next breath, metaphorically. The passage is in the first book, chapter 12. Augustine mentions that while he disliked Greek, he loved Latin, not the elementary studies in the Latin language but the more advanced readings in the literature. Now, in retrospect, Augustine says that his preference for literature over the fundamental considerations of language was folly: in the study of language you were concerned with straightforward things, and you learned how to read and write. Literature was misleading:

> nam utique meliores, quia certiores, erant primae illae litterae, quibus fiebat in me et factum est et habeo illud, ut et

legam, si quid scriptum invenio, et scribam ipse, si quid volo, quam illae, quibus tenere cogebar Aeneae nescio cuius errores oblitus errorum meorum et plorare Didonem mortuam, quia se occidit ab amore, cum interea me ipsum in his a te morientem, deus vita mea, siccis oculis ferrem miserrimus.

He might have learned, in his study of language, that it is possible to pass from error (wandering about) to error (immoral vagrancy), and from Dido's body dead to Augustine's soul dying of another separation. But nothing short of reading the *Aeneid* could have shown him how to maintain the tone of affectedly prejudicial comparison between "one Aeneas"—*Aeneae nescio cuius*—and a soul that knew itself hardly more intimately. Latin effects these transitions—as, in chapter 18 of the first book, Augustine seriously plays upon *pacta litterarum* and *aeterna pacta perpetuae salutis*—with such grace as to make similar transitions in English seem lurid.

WE HAD ALSO an anthology of short stories. You were free to read other fiction in your own time, and I read *Treasure Island, Kidnapped, Great Expectations, Pride and Prejudice,* and a heartbreaking book called *Lost Fields,* by Michael Mac-Laverty, which I was given as a prize at the end of some year. I recall most vividly Liam O'Flaherty's "The Reaping Race," although the moral of the story—that patience wins in the end—seemed inglorious. But I read these stories mainly to see how to write a sentence. The stories were too short; they closed upon their meaning with a snap, a finale delivered as if it waited to be applauded. Novels were better. Sometimes Mr. Crawford recited a passage and cackled to appreciate it, but his chosen passages were always sarcastic or otherwise dismissive. Was it from Theodore Dreiser's *The Financier* that he quoted a typical sentence: "He combined a Presbyterian conscience with an almost Asiatic perception of the main chance"? We knew what a Presbyterian conscience was, seeing specimens of it in every Protestant who passed by. What an Asiatic perception of the main chance was, or how it differed from the Occidental variety, was not clear. But it was the sentence itself that counted. What makes a good one? My sentences tended to run in threes: three clauses or three phrases. Three adjectives were excessive. The sole lesson I learned from Brother Cotter was that one adjective to each noun was enough and that it was wise to have some nouns free of adjectives. Adverbs were difficult, if only because their ending in -*ly* turned the sentence into a jingle.

The problem was: how to find something to say. Valéry somewhere remarks that fortune or chance gives the poet the first line of a poem, but you have to proceed from there on your own authority. I was never given a first line, but I felt that if I could beg, borrow, or steal one, something to write about, I could do the rest. Just the first sentence, and I'm off. In school, Mr. Crinion came upon the word *sententia* in Cicero and explained what it meant, then went further to explain how the meaning got into the English "sentence" and the legal meaning of "sentence" and how in turn it led to the adjective "sententious." It seemed to me wretched that something I admired, a well-turned sentence, should be punished for sounding sententious. Mr. Crinion said it was because a judgment or an opinion that expressed itself in a sentence was likely to be too sure of itself. He conceded that this made nonsense of law or of a legal opinion but explained that the law was allowed to express itself with a certain majesty; in ordinary speech or even in writing, such majesty would be offensive. I was not convinced.

Years later, when I got a job teaching in the English Department at University College, Dublin, my professor, Jeremiah J. Hogan, who wrote little but that little well, told me that the secret of writing good English was reading good Latin. His favourite prose writer was Cardinal Newman, and he maintained that Newman's clarity, even in difficult matters, was a consequence of his grounding in Latin. Newman could not have written *A Grammar of Assent* but for the precision and stability of Latin. When I told him that our students wrote badly and that it would soon be necessary to provide what in America were called, I believed, classes in expository writing, he expostulated: "Oh, no, no, surely it has not come to such a pass? The key is Latin and more Latin."

IT DID NOT OCCUR to me, in school, that sentences might not be the only form of statement or necessarily the best one. Not that I thought that they issued directly from nature or the hand of God, but I didn't question their being the entirely adequate expression of a perception. Nor did I think that there might be any other possibilities of the mind beyond that of perceiving. I knew that sometimes a part of the sentence could be left out; the omitted bit "was understood," as Brother Cotter said. When Keats writes, in the "Ode to a Nightingale," "Already with thee!" we understood that he meant: I am now with thee. That was acceptable, because he had been talking of flying to the nightingale on the viewless wings of Poesy, and the swiftness of the imagination allowed him to overcome the dull brain and join the bird in its flight.

But I don't think I understood that my reverence for the sentence as a form expressed not just my pleasure in the official relation between beginning, middle, and end, but my desire to see life as already intelligible. I'm sure I felt, at least vaguely, that even if life had many other qualities, it started by being intelligible. Sentences acted on that assumption and developed it further. The idea of a complex sentence, as in Henry James, showed the thrill of seeing risks taken and in the end the ship coming majestically into port.

THOREAU GLANCES at a distinction, in the chapter called "Reading" in *Walden,* between the mother tongue and the father tongue. The mother tongue is oral, and we acquire it without effort: even nincompoops do. The father tongue is written, a more arduous achievement and a much greater one:

The one is commonly transitory, a sound, a tongue, a dialect merely, almost brutish, and we learn it unconsciously, like the brutes, of our mothers. The other is the maturity and experience of that; if that is our mother tongue, this is our father tongue, a reserved and select expression, too significant to be heard by the ear, which we must be born again in order to speak. The crowds of men who merely *spoke* the Greek and Latin tongues in the Middle Ages were not entitled by the accident of birth to *read* the works of genius written in those languages; for these were not written in that Greek or Latin which they knew, but in the select language of literature.*

The repetition of "brutes" and of "select" points to a fixation. Thoreau never thought it necessary to take a woman seriously or the forms of life she embodied. Women hadn't even the merit of being children of nature; they were life in its stupid forms, a gabble for untrained ears. When he speaks of being born again, Thoreau means as a man. The ideal form of communication is between two men or between one man and himself. The invidious distinction between the italicised *spoke* and *read* leads, in the next paragraph, to a corresponding distinction between oratory, ignoble of course, and the written word, the work of a genius unequivocally masculine; and to a further distinction between clouds and the firmament of stars behind them. Clouds come and go, are shapeless, casual things, but the firmament of stars is permanent; astronomers read them like printed words.

I don't recall, in my sense of language, any such stringency, but I am sure the authority of a written sentence and the authority of my father were one and the same. It never occurred to me to dispute that privilege or to imagine that there might be feelings for which sentences were inadequate. In one of his aphorisms Kafka says that for everything outside the phenomenal world, language can be used only as an approximation, an adumbration, because, corresponding as it does to the phenomenal world, language is concerned only with property and its relations. This is probably more to the point than we would like to admit. The only way I see of mitigating the constraint is by extending the meaning of "property," as English already does, to include not merely things owned but

*Henry David Thoreau, *Walden* (New York: Library of America ed., 1985), pp. 403–4.

qualities present, as in the properties of a gas or a metal. The thought that sentences might be useless for some needs did not occur to me in school, and when I started finding complaints about language as such, in T. S. Eliot and other writers, I felt dismayed.

TWO CONGENIAL FORMS of expression: the sentence, embodying fully, if only for the time being, whatever needs to be said; and the gesture, which points to something that doesn't need any explication. In *La Carte postale* Jacques Derrida expresses "a sudden wish to take a small census of pointed fingers in painting, there are so many, genre Virgin of the Rocks, other da Vincis, etc."* Offerings for his census: certain Byzantine mosaics in the Cathedral at Cefalu showing a divine finger pointing to an open book; St. John the Baptist in the Grünewald Crucifixion from the Isenheim Altarpiece, pointing to Christ on the Cross; the male nude in Picasso's early *La Vie* pointing to a woman holding a child in her arms; and one of Philip Guston's charcoal drawings featuring a man with cowled or masked head, his left index finger pointing to an open book in his right hand, the drawing called—what else?—*The Law.*

It is unnecessary to choose between these two felicities, language as gesture, gesture as language. For me, growing up involved reluctant assent to vacillation, coming to realise that there are occasions in life on which certitude is obnoxious.

*Jacques Derrida, *The Post Card,* tr. Alan Bass (Chicago: University of Chicago Press, 1987), p. 206.

Pater says in *Studies in the History of the Renaissance* that "the way to perfection is through a series of disgusts,"* but doesn't indicate that many of these disgusts are provoked by a sense of certitude that we know to be premature. I have not grown to like the experience of vacillation or to think better of myself by residing in doubt.

MY DISTASTE FOR OUTDOOR SPORTS caused a problem at school—Brother Newell never forgave me—but not at home. My father believed in fresh air and thought that my readiness to walk to Burren and back was a sign of good nature and good health. But he did not encourage me to play football or any other game. Games required the company of one's fellows, and he wanted me to live as if among aliens. Besides, look at Tim. His prowess as a footballer merely wasted his time and energy. College football was tolerable, and when Tim played in Croke Park for the Ulster Provincial College team, my father and I went to Dublin for the occasion. But Tim made the mistake of playing football also for the local Warrenpoint Gaelic Football team and found himself among older and rougher players than those in school. One of those matches put an end to his career as a footballer: a local thug kicked him and smashed the cartilege behind his kneecap. Brother Newell arranged that Tim would have ses-

*Walter Pater, *Studies in the History of the Renaissance*, ed. Donald L. Hill (Berkeley: University of California Press, 1980), p. 81.

sions of physiotherapy; but he did not recover his strength or speed. My father did not allege that there was a direct connection between Tim's success on the football field and his lackadaisical performance in the classroom, but he allowed such an inference to be drawn. Even the more civilised games—swimming, tennis, running—were matters of indifference to my father.

The best exercise was walking. Next best, cycling. From Warrenpoint to Tullow was a long day's cycle of 126 miles: 74 miles to Dublin, a further 52 to Tullow. My father and I did it twice a year. We averaged ten miles an hour on old upright Raleigh bicycles, stopped every two hours for a rest and tea. My father had yet another theory, that tea and bread and butter made the best meal on such a journey: anything more substantial would be too much. Along the road, we knew where to stop for tea; a café, a tea shop, a public house. When we got to Drogheda, we always made a visit to St. Peter's Church before taking tea in a nearby café. Every schoolboy knew that St. Peter's contained the head of Blessed Oliver Plunket, who was hanged, drawn, and quartered on July 1, 1681, at Tyburn, after a specious trial for treason. The martyrdom of Blessed Oliver was the most dramatic episode in Britain's persecution of Catholics in the years of the Test Act (1673) and the Titus Oates Plot (1678). My father was not especially devout, but he thought it negligent to pass St. Peter's without going in and saying a prayer at the side altar, where, it was understood, the martyr's head was preserved in the tabernacle. Oliver Plunket was the object of notable devotion in Ireland in my time. His progress toward canonisation started on December 9, 1886, when Pope Leo XIII declared him worthy to be venerated. On May 23, 1920, Pope Benedict XV pronounced him blessed. (He was canonised by Pope Paul VI in 1975, the first Irish saint since St. Laurence

O'Toole in 1226.) We took it for granted that every prayer said in St. Peter's in Drogheda would bring the day of Blessed Oliver's canonisation nearer, as it did.

After Drogheda it was a comparatively easy ride to Dublin. We always had a larger meal at the Cora Café in Parkgate Street, just outside Phoenix Park. The owner of the café, a fat, jolly woman, recognised my father on each visit and treated us well. She seated us at a corner table which was covered with thick plate glass: underneath, there were paper doilies in elaborate oriental patterns. The meal was always the same: fried eggs, bacon, sausage, and fried bread. And tea, of course.

Cycling from Warrenpoint to Dublin was not a great strain, but as soon as I had eaten the meal at the Cora Café, I began to have doubts about my ability to go farther. There were various possibilities. If I felt I could not do it, we could go over to King's Bridge Station and wait for the evening train to Tullow, putting our bikes in the guard's van. Or we could compromise, take the railway road as far as Sallins or Naas and catch the train there. My father always wanted to keep going, but he did not exert any pressure. I knew that it was best, a feat, to cycle the whole way and still get to Tullow before dark. It was a stiff haul for the first part of the road, nearly a continuous hill from Terenure to the sanatorium at Crooksling. But from Crooksling to Baltinglass was easy, easier still when we got to Rathvilly. From there on, my body recovered; the last mile was downhill. In no time at all we passed Byrne's Garage, into the square—a puny thing compared with Warrenpoint's square—passed the statue of Father Murphy, a political martyr of the Rising of 1798, down into Bridge Street, and there it was, "Martin Coady," the paint flaking off year by year but still an exultant copperplate flourish. My father always allowed me to be the first to go into the house, to make the excitement and the triumph appear to be chiefly mine.

I DON'T REMEMBER exactly when we got the wireless. It was a large object, the woodwork mahogany or made to look like mahogany, with a circular cloth-and-wire grille in the middle and the stations on a celluloid screen on top. When not in use, the screen could be pushed down, level with the woodwork. I scanned all the stations—Droitwich, Hilversum, London, Athlone, Belfast—but the clearest signal came from Athlone, the town closest to the exact middle of Ireland. We must have got the set before September 1939, because I recall hearing Mr. Chamberlain announcing in a frail, woebegone voice that Britain was now at war with Germany. I didn't regard myself as at war: as a Catholic, my loyalty was to Ireland, not to Britain, and I didn't consider Northern Ireland a part of Britain. But my father and I gathered around the radio every night to hear the BBC nine o'clock news on the progress of the war. I took it for granted that the British, unattractive as they were, spoke the truth, and that when the BBC announcer reported that Royal Air Force bombers had bombed some German city with great success, he was telling the truth. "All our aircraft returned home safely." It did not occur to me to suspect that this sentence, delivered in such forthright terms, might be a lie. From Athlone, Radio Éireann broadcast little plays, music, recitals of singers and instrumentalists, sketches of domestic life, Joe Linnane's *Question Time*. I was much impressed by a radio version of Frank O'Connor's "In the Train," about a group of villagers returning from Dublin, where they had perjured themselves at a trial rather than give up to the law one of their own. The sound effects, suggesting passage from the law's compulsion to the adversary truth of the villagers, were thrilling. Sounds off. "Words have been my only loves, not many." Joyce has a little poem which Brian Boydell set and I sang: "Strings in the earth and air . . . make music sweet." As indeed they do.

I WAS ILL AND REMOVED from school for a year. A shadow of some kind was discovered near a lung, so I was told to rest, stay as much as possible in fresh air. I spent much of the time reading, on fine days sitting on the garden seat outside the Crawfords'. Mr. Crawford had many books, and I had the run of his library. I read mainly novels, poems, and essays, and thought that an essay was a fine thing and that I might one day be able to write one if I had anything to say. It did not occur to me then or later that I might try to write a poem or a story: these were achievements of a different and far more mysterious order. Surely I could write an essay by putting one decent sentence after another one of much the same character, and send them walking forth as my father put one foot after another and walked handsomely. No special form or degree of imagination seemed to be required. Have a thought, then another one decorously in its train. It seemed not impossible. The only time I ever tried to write a story was when, in some essay, I came upon the word "tyke," meaning a low-bred dog, and I started thinking about different degrees of breeding in people and trying somehow to bring them together for the interest of the conjunction. But I failed to make the piece interesting even to myself, and gave it up. I acquired a taste, a relish, as the priests said, for the essay as a form, a curve of having something to say, a trajectory of seemly words.

Relish: on days of abstinence, when the Catholic Church forbade the eating of meat, it was permissible to cook fish, say, in oil derived from meat "to give the food relish." Can that be correct or have I recalled it inaccurately? "Relish" was the word; I remember that; "relish," not "savour." I recall another exactitude: on days of fast it was permitted to eat one full meal and two collations. There was some discussion about the nature of a collation: whether it was distinguished from a meal by virtue of its size, its minuscule character, or by virtue of its ingredients and composition. In our house the question was regarded as irreverent and trivial.

GIRLS: NO GRAND PASSION occurred to me in their company, though I could feel that they were a different order of reality, and an infinitely higher one, than boys. I recall mainly their names and the opulent lapse of one syllable into another. Camilla, Madge Crawford, Aileen, whose surname I have forgotten, though I recall the colour and sweep of her hair. Isabel Bridges; but that was a different provocation. During my ill year the local authorities laid a new maple floor in the Town Hall and opened it for roller-skating. The air of the hall could not have been regarded as fresh, but I was allowed to go skating and soon came to be good at it. So good that I could dance on skates as I never thought of dancing without them. Among the boys, I excelled. The best skater among the girls was Isabel Bridges, a girl who moved, at least on skates, like a queen. I wanted to dance with her, but it was out of the question. Her father was the local manager of the railway and a Protestant, so I could not think of speaking to his daughter. No matter now, but at the time it felt like deprivation. Not that in any formulated sense I disapproved of political or religious divisions. A Protestant was as alien to me as a Muslim, and Muslims had the merit that I didn't know any of them. It did not occur to me not to keep my distance. When we left Warrenpoint in September 1946 and went south, it was a new experience to cease distinguishing between Protestants and Catholics. I continued to know the difference and to deduce that Brian Boydell, say, was a Protestant, or at least not a Catholic. That was what a Protestant was to me. A Protestant was someone who wasn't a Catholic. In the South the distinction was and is a minor matter; it did not affect social life. Personal life it affected. Marriage between a practising Catholic and a practising Protestant was an awkward matter, requiring from the Protestant strict concessions about the faith in which their children would be brought up. But in ordinary social life, meeting Protestants was no longer difficult or embarrassing. The reason is simple. In the North the Protestants are masters; the Catholics are expected to know their inferior place. In the South the Catholics are so many and the Protestants so few that there is no conflict. After the Anglo-Irish Treaty some Protestants went to England or to Northern Ireland, and those who stayed assimilated themselves fairly easily into the new structures. There were problems. For the many years in which it was illegal to import into the South any device for birth control, Protestants had to make their own arrangements, presumably by an occasional trip to Belfast and a bit of smuggling on the way back. Catholics were forbidden, both by Church and State, to engage in such activities. But few Protestants made a public fuss about the denial of their rights. Divorce was the other issue. Divorce with the right of remarriage is illegal in

Ireland, mainly because the Constitution of 1937 is a document based upon Eamon de Valera's vision of a Catholic Ireland in which personal and sexual relations would be sanctified by marriage, and the structure of the family would remain forever intact. Yeats's famous speech in Seanad Éireann denouncing the proposed legislation banning divorce was animated by his conviction that since the Catholic Church, but not the Protestant Church, forbade divorce, the banning of divorce by the Irish Free State would further separate Protestants from Catholics and therefore the North from the South. Most of his Protestant colleagues in the Senate were dismayed by Yeats's arrogance in claiming to speak for them, and his association of Protestantism with the greatest names in the history of Ireland—Burke, Grattan, and the other eighteenth-century masters—did not gratify Protestant senators who wanted to get along in the Free State without unpleasantness. "We are no petty people," Yeats said, and with reason. His Protestant colleagues thought it a fine piece of oratory but in every other respect an embarrassment.

In more recent times governments in the South have produced, with remarkable ingenuity, "an Irish solution for an Irish problem"; it used to be called turning the blind eye. If your marriage collapses and you want to marry someone else, it behooves you to go to England or America for a while, get a divorce there, complete the marriage while safely abroad, and then come home without making any noise about your arrival. No policeman is likely to arrest you on a charge of bigamy. Let bygones be bygones. The question of property is another matter, but if you make acceptable arrangements in that regard, you are safe and sound.

Still, I wonder about Isabel Bridges. I hope she has continued to move through life with the walk of a queen. "The things that never can come back are several," according to Emily Dickinson. "Several" is an odd measure of one's losses;

either more than that or less, I would say. But Dickinson was judicious in her accounting. Sometimes I think the things that never can come back are innumerable; at other times, only a few. John, my brother, never can come back. That's as far as I want to count.

THERE IS A PASSAGE in the *Enquiry Concerning Political Justice* (1793) in which Godwin attacks the system of national education, on the grounds that it enforces the idea of permanence and unity, encourages a prejudice in favour of "such tenets as may chance to be established," and tries "to form all minds upon one model." I'm not sure whether he had in mind only the British system of education or presumed that every system of national education had the same—or a similar—prejudice. It may be true that every school has an interest in giving its pupils a conviction of permanence: it would be hard to imagine a school founded upon Heraclitean principles of change. And even Heraclitus sought, in the end, some stable principle beyond or behind the irrefutable appearances betokening change. Unity may be another question. It would be possible to imagine a school devoted to the idea of making its pupils at home in heterogeneity, teaching them to cope with differences and mobility. But I suppose most schools like to think of education as a comprehensive process, featuring at least an ideal unity of experience even if pupils mostly see indications of fragmentation. The division of knowledge into subjects isn't fatal to the inculcation of unity: if you divide something, you imply what you divide and posit it as unity.

In school at the Abbey I was aware of a certain social and political reservation, not in my mind but in the character of the school and the education it provided. The school was comfortable enough within the national system of education; it trained its pupils to sit for the state examinations and eventually for the Senior Leaving Certificate. It was not a private school; the teachers were paid by the State, and obeyed its instructions. On the other hand, the Christian Brothers did not feel any loyalty to Northern Ireland as a political entity. Government of the province was based on the propriety of "a Protestant parliament for a Protestant people," as its most celebrated Prime Minister described his ideal institution. The Christian Brothers did not encourage us to become rebels, but they recognised that a Catholic growing up in the North must live by a certain stratagem, spiritual secrecy. Everything done in the school was legal, but it was accompanied by the conviction that as Catholics we were by definition Nationalists. Our relation to the government at Stormont in Belfast was bound to be a withholding one, maintained by practising a double consideration. The centre of our universe, as Catholics, was Rome, the Church, its visible head His Holiness the Pope. Our aspirations as Irish boys were most fully articulated by the government in Dublin, even though its writ did not run beyond the Custom Post at Carrickarnon. Our sense of Stormont was therefore ironic. We were entitled to the benefits of British citizenship, a boon we had not chosen, but the Brothers took it for granted that we must enjoy these satisfactions with mental reservations. The Brothers did not expect that we would grow up to kill British soldiers or bomb public houses in Belfast, but they encouraged us to be spiritually and silently insurgent.

The teaching of Irish and of Irish history provided the richest occasions of this practice. Irish was a fully recognised subject in the official curriculum, though in practice it was taught mainly in Catholic schools. Learning Irish was therefore a sign that one's kingdom was not of the Protestant,

Unionist world; we lived elsewhere. That Irish and English were such different languages was a further token of spiritual secrecy: to speak Irish, it is necessary to speak differently, as if we were speaking French or Spanish; different pronunciation, intonation, cadence. It also entailed respecting and maintaining a form of social continuity which the British Empire and the Irish Famine of the 1840s had nearly ended. Under the Penal Laws in the eighteenth century, the Irish language was nearly defeated; it sustained itself only in remote communities along the Western seaboard. After the Famine, surviving parents knew that their children would have to leave the country or starve; and that if they left, they would have to speak English in their new countries: America, Canada, Australia. Besides, Irish was now associated with misery and defeat, the mark of a dejected people. In the middle years of the nineteenth century the British government did not have to destroy the language; it was already beaten. In the twentieth century those teachers who wanted to recover the Irish language taught it as a sacred trust, a difficult language, since its grammar and spelling were erratic and it existed in three main dialects. In Newry we learned the Irish of Ulster and spent a month in the summer speaking it and listening to it in Donegal.

Rannafast was the village in Donegal to which we were sent: it was and is a barren landscape, a stony place except for the few houses which survive largely upon the college. Every summer, hundreds of schoolchildren attend Coláiste Bhrighde, St. Brigid's College, taking classes in Irish language and literature. They live in the houses of native families where Irish is the spoken vernacular. It is doubtful whether the language can sustain itself against the force of television and transistor radios: in principle, these villages in Donegal (or rather in the Donegal Gaeltacht, where Irish is the daily language, as distinct from the Galltacht, where English is spoken) are supposed to be protected communities. The Irish government gives the villagers money, grants for improving their houses and services, in the hope of keeping them in Donegal, Connemara, and Kerry, where they provide at least a residual context for Irish as a spoken language. But the lure of foreign places is keen. The next generation will probably leave these communities and find jobs in Dublin or abroad. But in my time Rannafast was still a genuine Gaeltacht, and to some extent it still is. The college provided formal classes and entertainment in the evenings. When I was a student there, I went round to the houses where the best storytellers, the breed of *seanchaidhe,* were known to live, and transcribed their stories into my copybook. Irish was one of my best subjects, the supreme moment of my achievement in it being the speech I gave, at an *Oireachtas* in Dublin, as representative of the North.

THE HISTORY of the English presence in Ireland, as I imbibed it at school in Newry, is a simple story. It begins with two warrior kings, Diarmuid MacMurrough of Leinster and Tiernan O'Rourke of Breifne. In 1152 Diarmuid abducted Tiernan's wife, Dervorgilla, or, as the historian Keating maintained, Diarmuid allowed himself to be seduced by her. Tiernan took her back the following year, but he vowed to destroy Diarmuid. In August 1166 Diarmuid, defeated by Tiernan, escaped to England; he landed at Bristol and then sailed for France to sue for support from Henry II, King of England. Henry was a Norman, and his empire included not only England but much of France. Diarmuid promised him fealty if he would invade Ireland and restore him to his former power.

The King authorised Diarmuid to recruit an army from his Norman subjects in Wales. In the event, the leader of the Normans, Richard Fitz-Gilbert de Clare, known to us as "Strongbow," agreed to raise an army and invade Ireland on condition that Diarmuid gave him his daughter Aoife in marriage. In 1167 Diarmuid set sail with an army of Normans, Flemings, and Welsh. Beaten back at first by Tiernan, even to the extent of having to pay him one hundred ounces of gold in reparation for the abduction of Dervorgilla, Diarmuid sent for reinforcements to Wales. The first invaders landed at Bannow Bay in May 1169. Diarmuid joined them and marched on Wexford. On August 23 Strongbow arrived and set out for Waterford. Dublin fell to his forces on September 21, 1170. In October 1171 King Henry arrived at Waterford and took possession of the most fertile parts of the country, the province of Leinster, with Dublin as its city. From that day to this, Ireland has never been free of the English.

YEATS'S DANCE PLAY, *The Dreaming of the Bones,* is set in 1916. A young soldier who has fought in the Easter Rising has escaped from Dublin and is on the run in a hilly place between Clare and Galway. He meets a girl and a strange man; the girl tells the soldier that the shades of Diarmuid and Dervorgilla wander the hills but cannot kiss because

> . . . *when he has bent his head*
> *Close to her head, or hand would slip in hand,*
> *The memory of their crime flows up between*
> *And drives them apart.*

The crime is not adultery, but recourse to a foreign king:

> *Her king and lover*
> *Was overthrown in battle by her husband,*
> *And for her sake and for his own, being blind*
> *And bitter and bitterly in love, he brought*
> *A foreign army from across the sea.*

The girl explains that Diarmuid and Dervorgilla may come together for all eternity, but only if one of their race forgives them. Gradually it dawns on the soldier that the girl and the stranger are the shades of Diarmuid and Dervorgilla, begging his forgiveness. But he refuses:

> *O, never, never*
> *Shall Diarmuid and Dervorgilla be forgiven.**

With the crowing of the cock, the shades dance their agony and fade unappeased, unforgiven, into a cloud.

The setting of the play in 1916 has sometimes been thought gratuitous, but, as Peter Ure has noted, the Easter Rising may be thought to "aggravate the torment of conscience in which the lovers have 'lost themselves.'" The Rising, and the destruction of great houses and castles, "must be recognised as the direct consequences of the sin committed seven centuries ago."† The shades of Diarmuid and Dervorgilla, discarnate spirits, appear before the soldier of 1916 for that reason.

As a consequence of Diarmuid and Dervorgilla, a country in its essential character Gaelic and Catholic has been occupied, according to the Christian Brothers, by a foreign element, the English. One of the crucial stages of that occupation

---

*W. B. Yeats, *Collected Plays* (London: Macmillan, 1952), pp. 441, 442.
†Peter Ure, *Yeats the Playwright* (London: Routledge and Kegan Paul, 1963), p. 95.

was the Plantation of Ulster, an arrangement by which, in the first forty years of the seventeenth century, mercenaries of the British Crown were paid not in money but in land, seized from the native Irish in the Northern counties. As a result, English and Scots Presbyterians and their descendants have dominated the North. England's power over Ireland—the entire island—culminated in the wretched Act of Union between Great Britain and Ireland, which came into force on January 1, 1801. In every generation since 1798—the year of the French invasion—a few heroic men have banded together and risen against the Crown, with little hope of victory but determined to keep the flame of freedom alive. These rebellions were brutally put down and their leaders executed or transported in convict ships to Australia. On Easter Monday 1916 Padraig Pearse and a handful of men took over the General Post Office in Dublin and proclaimed the Irish Republic, *Poblacht na hÉireann*. In a few days they were defeated; a few weeks later, executed. But the flame of freedom could not be extinguished. In 1921 the British government was forced to concede to the Irish people a partial recognition of their claim: independence for twenty-six of the thirty-two counties. The remaining six were handed over to the Unionists, descendants of the Planters.

The logic of this story was not enforced by the Christian Brothers, but a Platonic version of it was clear. Ireland had not yet achieved its freedom. But in the fullness of a better time the country would be united; we would be "a nation once again."

The Christian Brothers did not urge us to prepare ourselves, in any militant sense, for the glorious day. There was no question of joining the Irish Republican Army, a body that barely existed except for a few irreconcilables who expressed their dissidence by wearing a lily on Easter Monday. But we were encouraged to regard the history of Ireland as unfinished business, a great story that lacked only a noble resolution. It was our duty to maintain a sense of Ireland, to learn the language and speak it, take part in national and never in foreign games, practise the old customs of Ireland, and above all keep alive the great consanguinity between Ireland and the Catholic Church.

In practice we defined ourselves by not doing certain things. We stayed clear of English games—soccer, rugby, cricket, hockey—and played, if any game at all, Gaelic football or hurling. Catholic girls played *camogie,* a modest version of hurling. We took part in *féiseanna,* the Irish for festivals, which featured Irish music, vocal and instrumental. I won a medal at a *féis* in Newcastle for singing in Irish, but failed to win any prize in a competition for instrumental music; my performance on the violin, especially in traditional Irish music, was poor.

At those *féiseanna* it was permissible—or at least it was not illegal—to play or sing Irish songs, with the single exception of "The Soldier's Song," which was and is the national anthem of Ireland. To express our kinship with the spirit of Ireland, we sang and bands played such songs as "The West's Asleep," and "A Nation Once Again," and nationalist ballads like "The Croppy Boy." "A Nation Once Again," written by Thomas Davis, the leader of the Young Ireland movement and, in 1842, founder of the *Nation,* became for us an unofficial national anthem. When a pipe and drum played it at the *féis* in Newcastle, every movement in the field stopped and we stood to attention:

> *When boyhood's fire was in my blood,*
> *I read of ancient freemen,*
> *For Greece and Rome who bravely stood,*
> *Three Hundred men and Three men.*
> *And then I prayed I yet might see*

Our fetters rent in twain,
And Ireland, long a province, be
    A Nation once again.

And, from that time, through wildest woe,
    That hope has shone, a far light;
Nor could love's brightest summer glow
    Outshine that solemn starlight:
It seemed to watch above my head
    In forum, field, and fane;
Its angel voice sang round my head,
    "A Nation once again."

It whispered, too, that "freedom's ark
    And service high and holy,
Would be profaned by feelings dark,
    And passions vain or lowly;
For freedom comes from God's right hand,
    And needs a godly train;
And righteous men must make our land
    A Nation once again."

So, as I grew from boy to man,
    I bent me to that bidding—
My spirit of each selfish plan
    And cruel passion ridding;
For, thus I hoped some day to aid—
    Oh! can such hope be vain?
When my dear country shall be made
    A Nation once again.

It was an embarrassment to the Christian Brothers that Davis, like many of the great exponents of Irish nationalism, was a Protestant. Daniel O'Connell was a Catholic, though a disreputable one, so he was the greatest hero since St. Patrick. But it was implied that, after the generation of Yeats and Synge and Lady Gregory—Protestants all, regrettably—the sentiments those writers expressed could be retained and transposed into Catholic terms. Ireland in its deepest character was a Catholic country. The fact that social conditions and a repressive foreign Crown prevented Irish Catholics from expressing the spirit of the nation was a disaster, but it might yet be undone by a new generation of well-educated and devout men and women. The Rising of Easter Week was the first rebellion to be planned and led by middle-class Catholics. Pearse was a Catholic, a teacher, a poet, a translator from the Irish:

> *I have turned my face*
> *To this road before me,*
> *To the deed that I see*
> *And the death I shall die.*

SINCE 1968 it has become fashionable to deride this account of Irish history. Revisionist historians have been undermining the Christian Brothers' version of our history. Many of them argue that the Easter Rising was a lamentable waste of blood and spirit. They assert that independence, for the South, would have come in its due time without a drop of blood spilled. If the Rising had not taken place, a British government in 1918, at the end of the Great War, would have set about implementing a much-promised and long-deferred Home Rule. Unionists in the North would have insisted on staying in the British Empire, but that was inevitable anyway. In the event, the Rising led to the Anglo-Irish War of 1919–21 and the bitterness of Civil War after the Treaty of 1921.

It has also been maintained that the leaders of the Irish

Literary Revival, and especially Yeats, bear much responsibility for the rise of the IRA and the bloodshed since 1968. Conor Cruise O'Brien has described Yeats's *Cathleen ni Houlihan* (first performed by the Irish National Dramatic Company on April 2, 1902, at St. Teresa's Hall, Clarendon Street, Dublin), as "a straightforward, red-hot piece of physical-force-nationalist propaganda." If someone were to put on a performance of the play "as a benefit performance in support of the Provisional IRA," O'Brien said, "they would not have to alter a single line."*

The play is set in Killala in 1798 on the day of the anticipated landing of the French. The plan is that the French will join with the Irish and march east against the English. Dedicating his play to Lady Gregory, Yeats wrote of it:

> One night I had a dream almost as distinct as a vision, of a cottage where there was well-being and firelight and talk of a marriage, and into the midst of that cottage there came an old woman in a long cloak. She was Ireland herself, that Cathleen ni Houlihan for whom so many songs have been sung and about whom so many stories have been told and for whose sake so many have gone to their death. I thought if I could write this out as a little play I could make others see my dream as I had seen it. . . .†

After the first performance Yeats described the play again:

> My subject is Ireland and its struggle for independence. The scene is laid in the West of Ireland at the time of the French landing. I have described a household preparing for the wedding of the son of the house. . . . Into this household comes

---

*Conor Cruise O'Brien, "An Exalted Nationalism," *The Times,* January 28, 1989.
†*The Variorum Edition of the Plays of W. B. Yeats,* ed. Russell K. Alspach (London: Macmillan, 1966), p. 232.

Cathleen ni Houlihan herself, and the bridegroom leaves his bride, and all the hopes come to nothing. It is the perpetual struggle of the cause of Ireland and every other ideal cause against private hopes and dreams, against all that we mean when we say the world.*

In the play, when the bridegroom is about to go with the old woman, she says:

> It is a hard service they take that help me. Many that are red-cheeked now will be pale-cheeked; many that have been free to walk the hills and the bogs and the rushes will be sent to walk hard streets in far countries; many a good plan will be broken; many that have gathered money will not stay to spend it; many a child will be born and there will be no father at its christening to give it a name. They that have red cheeks will have pale cheeks for my sake, and for all that, they will think they are well paid.

In the last lines of the play, Peter Gillane says to his son Patrick, "Did you see an old woman going down the path?" and Patrick, a boy of twelve, answers, "I did not, but I saw a young girl, and she had the walk of a queen."†

Conor Cruise O'Brien's account of *Cathleen ni Houlihan* is fair, the little distance it goes in considering Yeats's entire work and its bearing upon Ireland past, present, and future. The play could indeed be performed to sustain the Provisional IRA. But the IRA thrives upon motives—nationality, Cathleen ni Houlihan, Mother Ireland—to which successive Irish governments, since de Valera came to power in 1932, have given mere lip service, keeping those motives notionally alive on the understanding that no one would act upon them. The

---

*W. B. Yeats, *The United Irishman,* May 5, 1902; reprinted in *The Variorum Edition of the Plays,* p. 234.
†*Variorum Edition,* pp. 229, 231.

rhetoric of Irish politics since 1932 has been a cynical exercise in bad faith. It is dishonourable for Irish governments to persist in a claim upon the unity of Ireland and to make that claim—in relation to the British government—with studied silence. The Anglo-Irish Agreement, signed on November 15, 1985, by the prime ministers of both countries, Margaret Thatcher and Garret Fitzgerald, guaranteed that the constitutional status of Northern Ireland will remain unchanged unless and until a majority of the people of the North signify their wish to join with the South in a united Ireland.

In effect, revisionist historians are asking Irish people to forget about nationality or to seek a new role in membership in the European Community and other such bodies. Conor Cruise O'Brien does not see any contradiction between his repudiation of nationalism in Ireland and his writing *The Siege*. Nationalism is a fine flower, so long as it grows in Israel, Tibet, Poland, and Lithuania.

THE NOTION OF PARTITION that I learned in Newry was seriously inaccurate. I grew up thinking that the division of Ireland into twenty-six southern and six northern counties was an arrangement imposed by Lloyd George upon the Irish delegates at the discussions leading to the Anglo-Irish Treaty in 1921, and that his insistence on immediate agreement to it defeated the Irish representatives. They had to go back to Dublin and report that the country was to be divided. This was not the case.

The idea of Partition was first raised in August 1911 in the context of the Home Rule Bill then in preparation. At that point there was talk of four counties—Antrim, Down, Armagh, and Londonderry—being exempted from Home Rule: they were to stay in the British Empire. In the event, the bill, introduced in April 1912, did not propose Partition, but in the form in which it eventually passed through the House of Commons in May 1914 on its way to the Lords, it allowed each of the northern counties to opt out of Home Rule for six years. The House of Lords changed this provision and allowed the nine counties of Ulster to secede without any limitation of time. When war was declared in August 1914, the Unionists committed themselves to it, determined to show their loyalty to King and Country. In the South, Nationalists took the view that the war was England's business, not Ireland's. When John Redmond, leader of the Irish Parliamentary Party at Westminster, offered to send the Irish Volunteers to fight side by side with the British Army in France or any other country, he split the soldiers. Those who supported him called themselves the National Volunteers; those who rejected his call became the Irish Volunteers and moved toward insurrection. To them, England's difficulty was Ireland's opportunity.

After Easter Week the split between Northern Unionists and Southern Nationalists was definitive. When the Great War ended, the British government set about securing the power of Unionism. The Government of Ireland Act, passed on December 23, 1920, set up two devolved parliaments, one (Stormont) in Belfast for six counties, one in Dublin for the remaining twenty-six. In the South the provisions of the act were largely ignored, but in Belfast the new parliament went into action at once. In fact, Unionists had been working in league with British civil servants in Dublin Castle to set up an administrative system in the North even in advance of the legislation to authorise it. To deal with the Southern Nationalists, Lloyd George had to choose between governing the South by martial law and offering to negotiate. He decided to negotiate.

There was no question of dismantling Stormont. Indeed, at that stage the separate existence of Northern Ireland was not a hanging matter. Many Nationalists in the South thought that, on balance, it was better to give the Protestant Unionists their own petty parliament than to have them included in a united Ireland, where they would be nothing but a nuisance. During the Treaty negotiations there was talk of setting up a Boundary Commission to determine, according to the disposition of the people in each area of the North, the exact form of Partition, the boundary on a map. Some people naively believed, or were cajoled by Lloyd George into believing, that the Boundary Commission would reduce Stormont's scope from six to perhaps four counties. If that were to come about, the North would be too small to survive as a separate entity, even on the assumption that Britain would support it financially. In the end the commission could not change the border or its constituencies: the Unionists would have taken up arms against any change.

The Christian Brothers did not explain the Treaty discussions. They did not tell us that only twenty-six counties were in question. What form was the new Irish Free State to take? In the event, the Civil War was not fought on the issue of Partition but upon a refusal of symbolism. The British insisted that members of the new parliament in Dublin would take an oath of allegiance to the British Crown. Extreme Nationalists, led by de Valera, refused. Those who supported the Treaty as a general document that could be worked and developed had no scruple about the oath. The Treaty was signed in London on December 6, 1921. On December 14 the debates on it started in the Dublin parliament (Dáil Éireann). On January 7, 1922, by a majority of 64 to 57 votes, it was ratified. On January 9 Arthur Griffith was elected President of Dáil Éireann. On January 16 the Provisional Government replaced the British administration in Dublin

Castle. On April 14 anti-Treaty forces seized the Four Courts in Dublin. The Civil War began on June 28, when the National Army, using heavy artillery provided by British forces still in Ireland, bombarded the Courts.

If Nationalists in the South were willing, in the years between 1911 and 1916, to think of Partition as a feasible means of recognising that Unionists in the North served a different God, it is hard to explain why, in my years at school in Newry, it was deemed a monstrous scandal. But the explanation becomes clear. By the time de Valera came to power in 1932, much had happened: the Easter Rising, the execution of Pearse and other leaders, the Anglo-Irish War, the establishment of the six counties with a separate parliament, the Treaty and its acceptance in Dublin, the Civil War, de Valera's defeat in that war and his laying down of arms, the years he spent in the political wilderness while the Free State Government was in office. In 1932 he came to power, but he needed a symbol, or at least a symbolic narrative. The separation of the six counties gave him such a narrative: in the Constitution of 1937 he identified the unity of the whole island as our cause.

ONE PROVISION of the Treaty had some importance for my little life in Warrenpoint. Britain retained the right, upon need, to occupy certain naval bases in the South; these were at Berehaven, Cobh, and Lough Swilly, with fuel storage at Haulbowline and Rathmullen. In 1938, as part of a trade agreement between de Valera's government and the British government, these ports were handed back. It was commonly assumed in England that if they were needed, they would be freely given. De Valera would allow the British Navy free and full use of the ports. That was an error of judgment. When de Valera and the Irish government decided to remain neutral during World War II, he regarded neutrality as having put the ports out of bounds to the British Navy. He also regarded neutrality as the definitive assertion of Ireland's sovereignty.

As a result, Northern Ireland was of immense strategic and defensive value to Britain during the war: it was used by British and American troops for that reason. Warrenpoint was a small town, but it was a port; it had a harbour—or at least Kelly's Coalyard—that could be enlarged to include a factory for the building of landing craft. Tim worked there as a welder.

A FEW YEARS AGO, the teaching of Irish history in schools throughout the country came under scrutiny. It was alleged by some revisionists that the modern IRA thrives upon sentiments inculcated by the teaching of Irish history as a continuous epic or tragedy of revolution. It was argued that Catholic schools in the North, and all schools in the South, should present the history of Ireland in social, economic, and cultural terms, rather than in terms of revolution and defeat. There was a proposal for a new textbook of Irish history, in four or five volumes, in which the main emphasis would be directed toward geography, economics, communications, transport, the history of the country as seen in its artifacts. The historian F. S. L. Lyons, the economic historian Louis Cullen, the architectural historian Maurice Craig, and I were to collaborate in the enterprise. After a few discussions the notion seemed to me artificial, its revisionist impulse too clear. The idea was not carried forward. But the most influential work in Irish historical studies in the past twenty years has played down the story of revolution and drawn more attention to the latitude of personal, social, and political experience which the history of Ireland entails. I am referring to the tradition of Irish historical studies as represented by T. W. Moody, Lyons, and Roy Foster.

There has also been a corresponding revisionism in the reading of Irish literature, and especially of Yeats's poems and plays. Seamus Deane and other Irish critics have argued that Yeats bears some responsibility for the violence in Northern Ireland because he presented the history of Ireland as a story of caste and kind, of peasant and nobleman linked by spiritual kinship through their living upon the land. Yeats was not interested in understanding Irish history in terms of class or social formations. His mythology was designed to transcend such considerations and to define the crucial relations, such as those of blood and race, spiritual forces which did not coincide with mere distinctions of class. As a result, Yeats's images of heroic life offer a grand destiny only to peasant and nobleman. The class which has come to power in Ireland—the bourgeois commercial or professional class—is despised in Yeats's poems. "Romantic Ireland's dead and gone." The rhetoric of Yeats's most powerful poems is animated by the emotion of tragedy, Nietzschean violence laughing in the face of death.

It is a difficult issue. On the one hand, it would be fatuous to think that poetry is by definition without power of incitement. "Did that play of mine send out certain men the English shot?", Yeats asked himself after the execution of the leaders of the Easter Rising. No one knows. Poetic images harbour a corresponding disposition to carry their energy into action. Among the rebel leaders in 1916, Padraig Pearse was imbued with a literary sensibility which fulfiled itself in heroic, blood-sodden images, motifs of Mother Ireland, and the book of crucifixion and resurrection. Among the current leaders of the Provisional IRA there is no sign of such a literary presence, though the speeches of Bobby Sands, who died on hunger strike, show something of the same imagery.

What the revisionist spirit in the reading of Yeats mainly shows is the reader's resentment. Seamus Deane resents the fact that, even yet, the development of Ireland has not proceeded in the classic Marxist way: the definition of social classes and formations, conflict arising from industrialisation, a trade-union movement, factory acts, technological change, and so forth. Except for the Lagan Valley, Ireland has never had an industrially defined history. There has never been, in the English sense, an Industrial Revolution in Ireland. The attempt by Bernadette Devlin to interpret the Troubles in Northern Ireland in neo-Marxist terms was specious: there is no context in which those terms find meaning and value, because there has not been any historical or social development to give them point and force. Seamus Deane is blaming Yeats for offering Irish boys and girls images of grandeur arising from consanguinities which take no account of socially defined classes. I see no merit in Deane's resentment, though much in him besides. It is the glory of poetic language that it impedes, even when it also solicits, the conversion of images into action. The purpose of its forms and ceremonies is to hold the reader's mind for as long as possible in a fictive or otherwise gratuitous space, where the relations are internal and not applicable. Images call to other images as in a little world made cunningly from its discovered formal and expressive possibilities. Above every poem or novel there should be a motto: "This road does not go through to action." A poem is not a tract, an editorial, or a sermon.

IN "The Work of Art in the Age of Mechanical Reproduction"—published in 1936—Walter Benjamin argued that the logical result of fascism was "the introduction of aesthetics into politics." Rather than set the masses free, Mussolini let them express themselves: circuses, festivals, marches, politics as spectacle. "All efforts to render politics aesthetic," Benjamin said, "culminate in one thing: war."* The statement is true but incomplete. To complete it, one should note that in 1936 many on the Left responded to fascism by introducing politics into aesthetics, thereby giving up the only remaining space of freedom. Their descendants are busy repeating the blunder.

I THINK I UNDERSTOOD, even at school, that whatever Ireland meant, the meaning disclosed itself in narrative terms. It might be true, as someone said, that the problem with Ireland and England was that the English could not remember and the Irish could not forget. Our meaning coincided with the narrative we inherited and commemorated. Revisionism is an attempt to alter the narrative or to imply that the official story, the myth or metanarrative, is false. But a myth is hard to dislodge, because its logic has taken a narrative form; to be compelling, a story does not need to be

*Benjamin, *Illuminations,* p. 241.

true. Lyotard has remarked that "narration is the quintessen-tial form of customary knowledge."* The history of Ireland, as I learned it from the Christian Brothers, was customary knowledge; it could lapse or congeal, but it could not, as a narrative, be refuted. A myth is a story told over and over again for the comfort of the community that receives it: its status apart from that community is of no account.

In *Major Trends in Jewish Mysticism* Gershom Scholem ob-serves that the social life of the Hasidim depended upon the wealth of their tales: the Torah took the form of "an inex-haustible fountain of story-telling." Nothing in Hasidism has remained theory or doctrine; everything has become a story. Here is one such story, as told to Scholem by S. Y. Agnon:

> When the Baal Shem had a difficult task before him, he would go to a certain place in the woods, light a fire and meditate in prayer—and what he had set out to perform was done. When a generation later the "Maggid" of Mes-eritz was faced with the same task he would go to the same place in the woods and say: We can no longer light the fire, but we can still speak the prayers—and what he wanted done became reality. Again a generation later Rabbi Moishe Leib of Sassov had to perform this task. And he too went into the woods and said: We can no longer light a fire, nor do we know the secret meditations belonging to the prayer, but we know the place in the woods to which it all be-longs—and that must be sufficient; and sufficient it was. But when another generation had passed and Rabbi Israel of Rishin was called upon to perform the task, he sat down on his golden chair in his castle and said: We cannot light the fire, we cannot speak the prayers, we do not know the

---

*Jean-François Lyotard, *The Postmodern Condition: A Report on Knowledge* (1979), tr. Geoff Bennington and Brian Massumi (Minneapolis: University of Minnesota Press, 1984), p. 19.

place, but we can tell the story of how it was done. And
. . . the story which he told had the same effect as the actions
of the other three.

To this, Scholem added a comment:

You can say if you will that this profound little anecdote
symbolizes the decay of a great movement. You can also
say that it reflects the transformation of all its values, a
transformation so profound that in the end all that remained
of the mystery was the tale.*

When we say that Ireland is a Catholic country, we mean
that most of its people have received their sense of the world
in narrative terms; the life, death, and resurrection of Christ,
the lives of the saints, the commemoration of Christ's life in
the sacraments, as elucidated by the teachings of the Church
through its doctrines and rituals. In Ireland, Sunday Mass is
the clearest form of customary knowledge. To the extent to
which this knowledge has been eroded, the erosion has come
about not mainly because of secularism at large but because,
for many people, narrative has lost its power. All that remains
of the mystery is the tale, and now, for those people, not even
that. "Lamenting the 'loss of meaning' in postmodernity," as
Lyotard says, "boils down to mourning the fact that knowledge is no longer principally narrative."†

---

*Gershom G. Scholem, *Major Trends in Jewish Mysticism* (New York: Schocken
Books, 1961 ed.), pp. 349–50.
†Lyotard, *The Postmodern Condition*, p. 26.

IT IS EASY to denounce the Christian Brothers for teaching a dangerous version of Irish history, and to point to the renewed violence in Northern Ireland since 1968 as the inevitable fulfilment of that pedagogy. It is true that any historical interpretation that features dramatic acts, unique individuals, and deeds of heroism turns life into theatre and violent men into tragic heroes. Bobby Sands saw himself in the light of the only history he knew. Social history is an attempt to remove from Irish history the glamour of its sacrifices and martyrdoms. Revisionism is a project of slow history, or confounding the drama, thwarting the narrative. Unfortunately, Ireland without its story is merely a member of the EC, the begging bowl our symbol.

I HAVE ALWAYS REGARDED Northern Ireland as an artifice. If it had succeeded, in the sense of maintaining itself economically and socially, it would have been a *tour de force*. But the reasons for its existence are merely opportunisms. It is true that, since the seventeenth century, there has been a concentration of Protestants in the region and that they have seen themselves as British rather than Irish. The fact that several Irish revolutionaries have been Protestants has confused the otherwise simple issue, and allowed some people to persuade themselves that the conflicts in the North have nothing to do with religion and everything to do with discrimination in jobs and housing. Protestants in the North think of the mother country as Britain, a confederation not precisely the same as England or even the same as the British Empire but as having its centre in London, specifically in the Queen. They think of Dublin as an alien place, the site of a sinister relation between Catholics and the Pope.

But the association between Protestants and Northern Ireland is not entirely accurate. At least since the eighteenth century, Protestants have lived with every sign of ease in virtually every county of Ireland. Protestant communities and parishes have not been confined to the North. The only significant difference between the North and the rest of Ireland is the fact that the North, or at least part of it, Belfast and the Lagan Valley, had something resembling an Industrial Revolution. The development of the linen industry in the North is one sign of that revolution; the shipyards of Belfast are another. These industries were dominated by Protestant families, with consequences not at all resembling the mode of life of Protestants living in the other counties of Ireland. There is an analogy between running a factory and governing a state: running a farm, teaching school, or owning a small shop in an Irish village is the source of a quite different imagery. In Tullow, my mother regularly angered my father by referring to two local gentlemen as Master Willie and Master Herbert. These were brothers named Burgess, a local Protestant family then falling not upon evil but upon powerless days. Their ancestors may have been powerful men; but even if they were, they would not have aspired to government. If the Burgess family had lived in the North, they would have run a factory or a large business or a professional firm; they would have seen themselves in an intimate relation to power. My mother called them Master Willie and Master Herbert because she was impressed by the character, however residual, of their family: the fact that they were Protestants made them objects of a more particular deference. Catholics were the same as we were; Protestants were different, not necessarily better but self-evidently different.

In describing Northern Ireland as an artifice, I don't mean that it can't last: it will probably last, mainly for artificial reasons. It is financially sustained by Britain, and even though Mrs. Thatcher and her government would like to see the entire island floating away in the general direction of Antarctica, they are committed to saving their faces by retaining the North. With every passing year, the reiterated desire of people south of the border to see Ireland united becomes an increasingly hollow sentiment. If we were asked: Do you wish to see Ireland united, the border removed, without the shedding of a drop of blood? most people in the South and the Nationalists in the North would say: Yes. Or rather: Yes, of course. The "of course" would testify to the long-unquestioned character of the "Yes." But if people in the South were asked: Do you think the Dublin government should maintain constant pressure, at the United Nations and in other venues, to get the British out of Northern Ireland and to dismantle the border at whatever cost? I don't think there would now be a majority in favour of that proposition. Since 1968 the North has become, in Southern eyes, a place to be wary of.

Nicholas Canny has argued, against the thesis that Northern Ireland was always a monstrosity—"a failed entity," as the *Taoiseach* Charles J. Haughey called it—that it might have succeeded but for certain developments in Britain:

> The unpalatable truth seems to be that the Partition experiment might well have worked if Unionist calculations, upon which discrimination in employment had been based, had not been upset by the extension of the benefits of the British welfare state to Northern Ireland. This enabled even unemployed Catholics, who might otherwise have been forced to migrate, to stand their ground against their per-

ceived local oppressors. The educational benefits of British welfare legislation also provided opportunities for deprived Catholics which they had not previously enjoyed, and facilitated the education of a new cadre of articulate Catholic politicians who exposed the shortcomings of the Unionist regime and thus undermined its credibility.*

Canny means, by that last reference, such politicians as John Hume, Bernadette Devlin, Austin Curry, and Paddy Devlin. These people were indeed the beneficiaries of the British welfare state, and they had the further merit of living in Belfast or Derry, coming together, especially in Queen's University, Belfast, to argue issues of the day. It was dismaying for Unionists to find that mere papists could be articulate and had to be heard.

THERE WERE SOLDIERS billeted in Narrow Water Castle, home of Captain and Mrs. Hall, less than a mile away from the barracks and Charlotte Street. The American troops were sloppy, they rarely seemed to salute their officers, and they walked along the street as if they despised their military routines. British soldiers were far better disciplined, though their rough uniforms made them appear, in comparison with the Americans, poor relations.

The British had ENSA touring companies, and they put on variety shows in the town hall every Saturday night when the skating was finished. It was all right to go to these shows provided I got out of the hall before they played "God Save

*Nicholas Canny, "Upper Ireland," *The London Review of Books,* March 16, 1989.

the King." To be caught standing to attention for the British national anthem was a terrible crime in my eyes. The company had two blond girls, made up to look like sisters. They played accordions while the lights were focussed to give the impression that, behind the accordions, they were nude. There was a diminutive comedian who played the saxophone. One of his front teeth was worn away, the enamel gone to blackness. He spent his days sitting on the long garden seat outside Maisie O'Neill's shop. One day he crossed to Omeath—it must have been a Sunday—to drink, and he was murdered, his body found the following day on the mountainside above the town. No one was ever arrested or charged with the killing.

Sometimes the soldiers, especially the Americans, joined in the skating. No Catholic would speak to them or acknowledge that they were in the hall. But some of the Protestant girls would laugh and skate with them. It was their war, not mine. The Ireland I cared about stayed neutral. De Valera's explanation was that so long as Ireland remained partitioned, the country could not join with Britain in a common enterprise. But when Belfast was bombed by the Germans, on three occasions in April–May 1941, the Dublin government immediately sent five brigades north to help the wounded and to bring supplies: it was our city, by right.

THE SQUARE WAS a great place for parades, marches, exhibitions. Four days in the year had special significance and were observed with banners flying: two for Protestants, two for Catholics. The first was St. Patrick's Day, March 17, and pipe-and-flute bands, as many as twenty from Catholic villages and towns throughout the North, came to Warrenpoint and marched around the town, the banners in gold and green. Then, on July 12, the famous "Twalfth," Protestants arrived in similar numbers and gallantry, with banners commemorating the great and glorious victory of King William over the wretched James at the Battle of the Boyne in 1690. The banners showed the King crossing the river, victory in his crest. Protestants, mostly Orangemen, turned out for the march in black suits and hard black hats. The Catholics turned out again on August 15, Feast of the Assumption of Our Blessed Lady. Protestants answered back on the last Saturday in August, Black Preceptory Saturday, as it was called for no reason that I know. Someone told me that it had to do with the Freemasons or the Knights Templar.

These processions were indeed rival occasions, but they were not occasions of violence. Catholics watched the Protestant processions from the sidewalks but did not interfere with them or make any audible noise. Similarly with Protestants on the Catholic days. In any strict sense, the "Twalfth," as we mimicked the Protestants in calling it, was the most aggressive of those days, the only one that specifically celebrated the historic victory of a Protestant King over a Catholic Pretender. The other Catholic days were days of religious celebration, but even St. Patrick's Day didn't mark a victory of Catholic over Protestant; and the Assumption of the Blessed Virgin was entirely a matter of Catholic belief and practice; it had nothing to do with Protestants.

A few Catholics took the occasion of Easter Monday to celebrate the Easter Rising, but there was never a procession or parade: the memorial was an individual matter, its only sign the wearing of a paper lily in colours of green, white, and gold. To wear an Easter lily on Easter Monday was regarded by the authorities as a gesture extremely hostile to the state of Northern Ireland and therefore flagrantly offensive. It was also illegal, since, by virtue of the Flags and Emblems

Act, it is illegal to fly the flag of any nation in Northern Ireland except that of the British Empire, the Union Jack. Since the South has never had diplomatic relations with Northern Ireland, the question of flying a tricolour, the green-white-and-gold of Ireland, in Belfast or elsewhere has not arisen. But anyone who wore the Easter lily knew that he was making a provocative statement. I am sure that my father, as sergeant, took the names of those he saw wearing the lily, but I don't think he prosecuted any of those dissidents. Equally, it was illegal to sing the national anthem of a foreign country in Northern Ireland, except upon an officially recognised occasion. If a Catholic, passing a Protestant, started singing or whistling "The Soldier's Song," it would be taken as an offensive act. But these provocations were rare. Most people in Warrenpoint were content to keep to themselves and to their own kind, letting the other crowd do the same.

THE FIRST TIME I met a complex situation, one that called forth simultaneously two contradictory responses, was the Sunday morning on which the military band of the Cheshire Regiment marched and played in the square. The music was stirring; a soldier at the head of the band marched leading a beautiful white goat, the regiment's mascot; the band contained the first glockenspiel I ever heard; the boots of the soldiers gleamed in the sunshine. But it was a British band, and Warrenpoint was Ireland and I was Irish and I hated to see the British soldiers in possession of an Irish town. Orangemen parading on the "Twalfth" were Irish, I believed, in some barely definable sense. One might equivocate on such an issue. Wolfe Tone was a Protestant, after all, and a better

Irishman than most, or so I was compelled to believe. But a regiment of the British Army parading around the square on a Sunday morning could not be talked away.

SMELLS: I HAVE A POOR sense of smell. A perfume has to be nearly wanton before I advert to it. Only one smell persists from the barracks: the disinfectant, Jeyes' Fluid. From our house: only the damp linoleum on the table.

Outside the barracks, another smell. My father and I are cycling to Tullow. We stop for tea at a public house or a tea shop every twenty miles. Somewhere between Drogheda and Balbriggan there was a shop, a general store, where we got tea and bread. On one of our trips, when we were putting our bicycles against the whitewashed wall of the shop, a bread van arrived and the driver opened the van and started unloading a tray of fresh bread. Pan loaves: the bread was hot and soft and the smell was of well-being and fellowship.

NARROW WATER WAS and is a castle, a large "modern" one in the great estate of woods and fields between Warrenpoint and Newry. It is also the remains of an ancient castle on the narrowed northern shore of Carlingford Lough. My father was on good but not familiar or easy terms with Captain Hall. Two or three times a year, the captain gave my father permission to shoot a deer on the estate. I was always in attendance, following my father a yard or two behind, holding my breath and walking softly lest I startle the deer. It seemed uncanny that a deer appeared, often on the brow of a hill, at once bold and vulnerable against the rim of the sky. Sometimes my father's first shot was enough, but not always; if the deer was only wounded, we had to track him through the trees as he leaped ahead and stumbled at last and we came upon him, still breathing. A second shot, this time to the head, finished him: the deer died with two or three spasms. My father had a hunting knife, and he cut up the carcass there and then. It was during the war, and meat was rationed, so I knew the taste of venison before that of the diamond-bone steak the butcher saved for my mother, whom he liked. She was the worst of cooks, but she was a provider. The butcher indicated, in his gruff way, that he would not let her down or see her short of a bit of meat. Like my father, my mother believed that it was not a meal unless it had meat and boiled potatoes.

AT SCHOOL, in the new school on the hill, I was accused of stealing a fountain pen. I sat at the same desk with Gerard Manley, and he owned a Conway Stewart fountain pen, brown with black stripes. It had a gold nib. If you held it up to the light, you could see the progress of the ink because the barrel was made of some faintly translucent stuff. One day, the teacher, Dan White, told me to collect the copybooks, and as soon as I started making the round of the class, Gerard Manley left the desk and went up to say something to Mr. White. When I had collected the copybooks, I handed them over to Mr. White, and he told me that Gerard Manley claimed that I had stolen his pen. Manley had a thin, dainty body and a sharp face. He looked at me as if he could see into my soul. I had not taken the pen. I had no idea where it was. I was quite willing to stand and have my pockets searched, and my schoolbag, and my overcoat in the cloakroom. But the pen was missing and never turned up. I could not be found innocent, in the absence of the pen. Nor guilty, though there might be a presumption of guilt, since only Gerard and I shared the desk. I had often seen the pen, and coveted it, because I hadn't got a fountain pen, only a Waverley pen that needed to be inked every few seconds. So in my heart, maybe I did everything but commit the theft.

LIKE EVERY OTHER BOY, I intended to live forever and saw no reason why I should not. Apart from that, I had no particular ambition.

MY FATHER WAS the rock of ages. So long as he was not called upon to bend or sway or compromise or turn the blind eye, he was superior to every condition he had to meet. But he was implacable. Rules were made to be kept. When Tim, to show bravado, came home a few minutes later than the prescribed eleven o'clock, he caused a scene; it was always the same scene: raised voices, anger, threats. In bed I hid my head under the pillow and planned to kill my brother.

I wanted my father to remain supreme, never to be at a loss except for words. The words didn't matter, so long as truth was maintained by my father's body and carriage. I sensed that the imperative duty, in my father's life, usurped every other gratification. I wanted to see him enjoy himself, not swaying in the wind but deciding to move equably to its rhythm. I wanted him to be lenient to himself, even if he could not be lenient to us, from a position of known strength. My father, to the best of my knowledge, never read a novel, never went to a concert or a film or a play. There was no space in his life that was not occupied with a purpose. His most resolute purpose was to provide for his children a better life than his own. There is a passage in *Conversations on the Good Uses of Freedom* where Grenier says that while it is a matter of chance whether one is born the son of a shoemaker or the son of a man of property, there are societies in which this hazard of nature is ratified; it is thought best that a peasant's son should remain a peasant. Why is this the case "if not in order to avoid the agony of choice"?* The custom has the further merit of preventing chaos. I suppose it accords, too, with the Elizabethan sentiment, itself of long standing, that a child should grow up and live and die in the place of his birth.

My father had no reason to think well of the social dispositions made available to him. An intelligent boy, he received virtually no formal education. He conceded that he had managed to surpass his origin. But he was not content. He was determined that his sons would not have to become policemen or his daughters the wives of policemen. How to achieve this? By education, which he grieved to lack. Education, examinations passed with honour, degrees obtained, and then a pensionable job, preferably in the Civil Service.

I had no objection to this plan or indeed to the predomi-

---

*Jean Grenier, *Conversations on the Good Uses of Freedom,* tr. Alexander Coleman (Cambridge, Mass.: Identity Press, 1967), p. 28.

nance of ambition in my life. I didn't know what form it should take or how it might be measured. In a fairly general sense, I felt—as my father did—that social life in Ireland and probably in other countries had a hierarchy of occupations, well recognised and accepted. The uneducated son of a mountainy farmer in Kerry was low on the social scale. A policeman was a good deal higher. The next level above a policeman was that of professional life: teachers, nurses, doctors, solicitors, bankers. Higher still were barristers, professors, medical specialists. It was unlikely that in one generation any of us could rise beyond the level of modest professional life. But the ambition was worthy in itself.

In Ireland such ambition was often regarded as a Protestant motive. Protestants worked hard, did well, got the best jobs. Catholics might or might not compete for the prizes. A vague sense of this distinction continues to obtain. The late F. S. L. Lyons was a gentleman as well as a scholar, and he was scrupulously fair-minded in all his activities. He knew Northern Ireland as intimately as he knew Dublin, where he lived for many years. But I always got the impression, from conversations with him, that he regarded the Northern tradition of Presbyterianism as bringing forth the best elements in Irish life: decency, sobriety, hard work, a determination to get ahead. The Catholic tradition, he thought, was slack, idle, careless in important matters. He recognised that these defects might be accompanied by corresponding merits: charm, good conversation, good humour. But if it came to a choice, as it often did, he was at heart a Presbyterian of the North.

I did not give much thought to the form of my ambition. From my father I learned to revere the law, even though it was British law and therefore in local respects alien to me. But law as such was thrilling. I saw myself among the intricacies of statute law, immersed in precedents, thrust and counterthrust. When I came as a student to University College, Dublin, I wanted to read law and become a barrister. Nothing in *Guide to Careers* indicated that it would be financially impossible, as it turned out to be. After the first week in Dublin I knew that only sons and daughters of the rich could aspire to become barristers: the costs were outlandish, and even if one managed to gain a degree of barrister-at-law, one had no guarantee of making a living. Unless one's family was in law, as another family might be in medicine, there was no hope of gaining access to it. I gave up the ambition and settled for an arts degree in English and Latin.

My only relation to the law was the experience of going to the petty sessions, held in the Town Hall, to hear my father giving evidence. He was a formidable presence in the witness box, answering questions with an exact sense of decorum. The Resident Magistrate, Major McCallum, listened to my father's evidence and invariably gave judgment accordingly. It never occurred to my father, or therefore to me, that the law was a man-made institution or that it was subject to change.

WHEN THE WAR STARTED, my father was instructed to round up and bring to Belfast for internment all "enemy aliens" who lived in Warrenpoint. An enemy alien, he explained, was a citizen of any country with which the Allies were now at war: a German, for instance, or an Italian. There were no Germans in Warrenpoint, so far as I recall, but there was an Italian family who ran the local fish-and-chip shop, Malocca's. The real name of the owner was Antonio Magliocca; Tony, to everyone who bought a bag of chips or an ice cream. My father explained the ordinance to Tony, and they agreed on a mutually convenient date for the internment. Tony was brought in a hired car from his shop in the square to Crumlin Road Jail in Belfast, where he sat out the war. I was brought along for the trip, my first sight of Belfast. I sat in the front for the view. Tony didn't seem to resent my father's part in the internment. On the way up to Belfast, he chatted with my father and maintained that the war would not last long.

MY FATHER DIED in the house in which I assume I was born. It was his custom, once a year, to dip his sheep. His procedure was to set aside one corner of the field we owned on the Carlow Road and to improvise a barrier or a railing. He filled an old bath with the appropriate disinfectant and rounded up the sheep—about thirty of them, as I recall—driving them into the corner area. Then he closed off the corner and started the dipping. This involved catching up the animal, dipping it under the disinfectant in the bath, and releasing it to the field. A man of sixty-nine should not risk the strain of this work unaided, but my father was headstrong, always reluctant to seek or hire help. Besides, he thought there was nothing beyond his powers. In the evening, when he had dipped all the sheep, he walked back to Bridge Street and went to bed. He died during the night.

I heard of it the next day. We were on vacation in Derrynane, living for a month in a converted boat house owned by the O'Connells, descendants of the Liberator, Daniel O'Connell. Every morning we carried buckets of drinking water from a pump about half a mile up the road to the Big House.

Every evening I took the toilet buckets and a spade and buried the excrement in the sand far out beyond the jetty at low tide. One evening, Frances called to me, waving a telegram. When I had finished the disposal business, I went up to the house and read it: "Father died this morning. Kevin." Kevin is Kathleen's husband, Kevin McGarry.

MY YEARS IN WARRENPOINT were neither happy nor unhappy. The question of one's happiness did not arise, mainly because, except in the matter of work and ambition, we were discouraged from asking large questions. I found it humiliating to be awkward, too tall, lanky, bad at games and athletics, especially in comparison with Tim's prowess. But it was easy to despise these activities and live an internal life of phrases and cadences. It didn't trouble me that the internal life was a tissue of quotations and allusions, the intelligence of other minds. Sometimes I felt that I had been born old and that I would never coincide with my time. I was posthumous even to my dreams, which I always failed to remember. I read *The Interpretation of Dreams,* but the book meant nothing to me, my dreams being already bleached by first light. Perhaps I chose to be born old and to forget the moment of that choice; chose, the better to resemble my father.

Kafka told Gustav Janouch that while the revolt of the son against the father is one of the perennial themes of literature, it is mostly shadowboxing. Of *The Playboy of the Western World,* Kafka said, "The son is an adolescent exhibitionist who boasts of having murdered his father; then along comes the old man and turns the young conqueror of paternal authority into a figure of fun." Besides, "Age is the future of youth, which sooner or later it must reach. So why struggle? To become old sooner? For a quicker departure?"* This from the author of *Letter to His Father*, a whine, addressed to one whom the son accused of having kept him down.

Besides, Kafka's reading of *The Playboy* is not accurate. At the end of the play Christy has dominated his father, and they go off together in league against the world. Old Mahon is delighted that life has made a man of his son at last, no longer the snivelling creature he was at the beginning. Freud has caused much mischief among families: young boys grow up thinking that the only way they can develop into manhood is by at least figuratively sleeping with Mother and killing or at least displacing Father. In the teaching of literature, Harold Bloom, too, has worked damage, if not mischief, by prescribing the Freudian "primal conflict" of son against father as the only way in which a strong writer develops his powers. A writer becomes strong, according to Bloom, only by displacing or circumventing the father, a figure at once chosen and destined to be chosen. A writer remains weak if he doesn't engage in such conflict. A very questionable theory, since it entails calling T. S. Eliot, for instance, a weak poet because his diverse relations to Dante and Shakespeare and Tennyson and Whitman were not entered upon as primal conflicts. It is absurd, I maintain, to claim that Eliot was weak and Stevens strong because Stevens's relations to Emerson, Whitman, and Pater were supposedly conflicts seized by Stevens for the testing of his powers.

I felt that my father was not only a strong man but the source of strength for me. Not strength to be developed in me by conflict. He was to me an example, an image; it was sufficient that I contemplated it, and not at all necessary for

---

*Gustav Janouch, *Conversations with Kafka: Notes and Reminiscences,* tr. Goronwy Rees (New York: New Directions, 1971), p. 69.

me to vie with its power. Merely by looking at him or by watching him as he crossed the square, I saw that it was possible to be fearlessly at large in the world. I imitated him, as a devout Christian lives by imitating Christ, not by challenging his authority or by strutting in his presence.

MY MOTHER RAN AN ACCOUNT at Curran's and settled it on the last day of each month. A green notebook contained enough detail to mark the transactions: the date, item, price. Regular items: sausages, tea, sugar, shoe polish, matches, eggs, peas, bacon, soup, jam, cocoa, marmalade, soap. On May 17, 1946, for the first time since the war started, she was able to buy bananas, costing two shillings and seven pence: the number or weight of the bananas, not noted. Every month, a receipt was gummed on the appropriate page of the notebook: 17 Church Street, Warrenpoint; for P. Curran, received from Mrs. Donoghue, Charlotte Street. To make the receipt impregnable, a two-penny postage stamp was fixed on it and endorsed with the signature of the receiving party. The last purchase was made on August 28, 1946, the only unusual item being a tea chest costing two shillings. It contained nearly all our possessions—my father having sold the piano, wireless, and mahogany table—when we left the barracks and Warrenpoint a few days later.

THE NORMAL AGE of retirement for members of the RUC was fifty-five. My father came to that age in 1942, but his service was extended till the end of the war.

In the months immediately after the war, I learned to enjoy being a spectator. Removed from school, I spent most of the time reading; in the parlour, as we called the living room, if the days were wet or cold; if warm, on the garden seat outside the Crawfords' or the one outside Maisie O'Neill's. The Crawfords' seat was better for reading, quieter. Maisie O'Neill's was better for watching the passing scene. The best seat was the high wall outside the barracks: from there one saw not only the traffic along Charlotte Street but across the square. From there I watched a victory display of low flying and formation flying by the Royal Air Force, an event that ended disastrously when two of the planes met and crashed over the square, one coming over Charlotte Street, the other coming from Burren. The plane coming from Burren broke up immediately, but the one that flew low over Charlotte Street nearly avoided the other, only to crash in the sea beyond the baths.

That last summer, for the first time, I saw my father vulnerable. A coal boat had docked, and the crew went to the nearest public house. One of them got drunk and started breaking the peace. My father was sent for. I was sitting on the Crawfords' seat, reading, and I saw my father walking toward the public house; in uniform, as always, steady. A few minutes later, I saw him scuffling outside the public house, trying to arrest the drunk man. They were wrestling on the footpath. My father was trying to handcuff the sailor but failing: the sailor was bigger, heavier than my father and, besides, drunk enough to be unmanageable. There were several men standing about, but none of them would go to my father's aid: in Northern Ireland nobody helps the police. In the scuffle my father's cap fell off. Without it he seemed to me a man like any other; his face and forehead lost their authority. He was just a man, his little, brief authority grappling with a sailor and failing to subdue him. I closed the book and clenched my teeth upon the leather spine and closed my eyes. When I opened them, I saw my father dragging the sailor by the feet across the square toward the barracks. It was all right. He had won, in a fashion.

My mother did not want to leave Warrenpoint, but we had no home to go to. Perhaps we could have stayed and found a house to rent. But I suspect that my father could not bear to go on living, without authority or uniform, in a town where he had been Sergeant Donoghue. In civilian clothes he seemed diminished. The obvious place to go was Tullow, where Ciss and Uncle Martin rattled around in a large, grim house and a farm of thirty acres quietly went to waste. I went to Dublin and found lodgings for a while at 99 South Circular Road, Kilmainham.

One piece of work remained unfinished. During the fourteen years in which, after John's death, we lived in Warrenpoint, my father did not arrange to have the child's grave marked by a headstone. It was a bare grave with a concrete surround; there was no name. Even when we left Warrenpoint, the grave at Burren remained without a marker. Neither my father nor my mother gave any indication that something remained to be done. Many years later, when both were dead, Kathleen made the necessary arrangements. John's grave is marked now—a piece of marble, his name, the date of his death. May thinks I have mistaken the year and that it should read: December 28, 1933.

But the question of my father matters. I can't fathom why he did not arrange to have a headstone erected before we left or even after we left. There are many aspects of my father on which I am willing to be blank, but this one leaves me bewildered. If one of my children died, I can't imagine leaving the corpse in an unmarked grave. And my mother: she did not inaugurate any part of our lives. But surely she might have made an exception for dead John and marked his grave.

I KNOW THAT my father, as I describe him, is not a well-rounded character; he appears partial and brittle. What I denote as his straightness could easily, by a flick of the wrist, be construed as merely rigid, inflexible. I can't help that. I am bound to believe that he was as I remember him—no more, no less. He found it difficult to be expressive; he wasn't easy or flexible or buoyant. I don't believe that he was cold or unfeeling, but I can't produce chapter or verse to prove that he wasn't. He loved his children, I do not doubt, but we were left to deduce the fact from mainly negative evidence: that he was just to us and honourable to everyone. As evidence, it is not much. At the time, I did not feel that he lacked anything: to have had a different childhood, I should have had to imagine one. My father filled all the space. It may say something about me, rather than about him, that I needed from my father only what he gave me. The rest I could imagine, or find elsewhere, or do without.

St. Brelades,
Warrenpoint,
Co. Down,
19th August 1957

Dear Mrs. Donoghue and Family:

It is with feelings of the greatest sorrow I heard of the death of your dear Husband. May he rest in peace.

What happened to him at all? It must have been a great shock to you all.

Only too well do I know how you are feeling, and I sincerely hope that God will give you courage and strength to bear this heavy cross.

What a lovely feast-day to die on! Our Blessed Lady must have given him a big welcome.

There was not one man on this earth poor Henry thought as much of as Mr. Donoghue, so I hope they have met in Heaven by now. He also had his little son, John Francis, whom he loved so much, to meet him.

Now Dear Mrs. Donoghue, do try and keep up, even for the sake of your family who will be as heart-broken as you are at the loss of such a devoted Father.

With renewed sympathy to you all from all here, and assuring you of our prayers. May God bless you.

Yours sincerely,
Mary Smyth.

FROM *The Irish Times,* August 28, 1979:

The British Army said they lost eighteen soldiers in a Provisional IRA double landmine ambush yesterday evening by the side of Carlingford Lough. Yesterday's ambush came as a three-vehicle patrol of the Second Parachute Regiment, based at Newry, drove along the scenic dual carriageway between Newry and Warrenpoint. Three vehicles, believed to have been a tender and two Land Rovers, were just passing a hay lorry parked at the entrance to Narrow Water Castle, near Warrenpoint, when the first landmine exploded a few minutes before 5 p.m. The second blast came about half an hour later when ambulancemen, firemen, and police were already on the scene, trying to help the wounded and count the dead.

The Provisional IRA in south Down said in a statement that their campaign would continue until there was "a declaration by Britain of intent to withdraw from the North."

FROM *The Irish Times,* Thursday, April 13, 1989:

A bomb gang who killed a 20-year-old woman and injured 34 other people in Warrenpoint, Co. Down, yesterday were described by the RUC as "criminal murderers who are a menace to the entire community."

Miss Joanne Reilly died instantly when a no-warning van

bomb demolished the hardware shop where she was employed. The bombers' target was the town's heavily-fortified RUC station beside Heatley and Morgan's hardware premises at Charlotte Street. The police station escaped serious damage.

Although no paramilitary group accepted responsibility in the immediate aftermath of the death and destruction, the attack bore all the signs of a botched IRA operation. Telephone warnings about the bomb were received after it exploded.

The massive explosion caused extensive damage to many homes and premises in the town centre. Casualties were rushed to the Daisy Hill Hospital in Newry, where staff had been mobilised to deal with the emergency.

Most of the people taken to hospital had been cut by flying glass and other debris and were also treated for shock. Many of them were neighbours from Charlotte Street, where houses and other buildings along its 100-yard length suffered widespread blast damage.

Among the people treated for minor injuries were six policemen who were in the station. Part of the side perimeter wall was blown down and cars in the station yard were damaged, but the building, which has a steel reinforced roof and protective window shutters throughout, was not structurally damaged.

A NOTE ABOUT THE AUTHOR

Denis Donoghue was born in Tullow, County Carlow, on December 1, 1928. He took his B.A., M.A., and Ph.D. at University College, Dublin, and received an M.A. at Cambridge University, when he joined the teaching faculty. He was Professor of Modern English and American Literature at University College and currently holds the Henry James Chair of English and American Letters at New York University. His many notable works include *Ferocious Alphabets, We Irish,* and *Reading America.*